New Da

GW00630958

Edited by **Sally Welch**

May–August 2021

The Bible Reading Fellowship
15 The Chambers, Vineyard
Abingdon OX14 3FE
brf.org.uk

The Bible Reading Fellowship (BRF) is a Registered Charity (233280)

ISBN 978 1 80039 038 6

Cover image: Thomas Denny's (1993) memorial window to Sir Peter Scott, St John's Church, Slimbridge, Gloucestershire, UK © Peter J. Hatcher, Alamy Stock Photo
Illustration on page 145 © iStock.com/A-Digit

Distributed in Australia by:
MediaCom Education Inc, PO Box 610, Unley, SA 5061
Tel: 1 800 811 311 | admin@mediacom.org.au

Distributed in New Zealand by:
Scripture Union Wholesale, PO Box 760, Wellington
Tel: 04 385 0421 | suwholesale@clear.net.nz

Acknowledgements
Scripture quotations marked with the following abbreviations are taken from the version shown. **NRSV**: The New Revised Standard Version of the Bible, Anglicised Edition, copyright © 1989, 1995 by the Division of Christian Education of the National Council of the Churches of Christ in the USA. Used by permission. All rights reserved. **KJV**: The Authorised Version of the Bible (The King James Bible), the rights in which are vested in the Crown, are reproduced by permission of the Crown's Patentee, Cambridge University Press. **GNT**: Good News Translation in Today's English Version – Second Edition Copyright © 1992 by American Bible Society. Used by permission. **MSG**: *The Message*, copyright © 1993, 1994, 1995, 1996, 2000, 2001, 2002 by Eugene H. Peterson. Used by permission of NavPress. All rights reserved. Represented by Tyndale House Publishers, Inc. **NIV**: The Holy Bible, New International Version, Anglicised edition, copyright © 1979, 1984, 2011 by Biblica. Used by permission of Hodder & Stoughton Publishers, an Hachette UK company. All rights reserved. 'NIV' is a registered trademark of Biblica. UK trademark number 1448790. **NLT**: The Holy Bible, New Living Translation, copyright © 1996, 2004, 2007, 2013. Used by permission of Tyndale House Publishers, Inc., Carol Stream, Illinois 60188. All rights reserved. **NEB**: The New English Bible, copyright © Cambridge University Press and Oxford University Press 1961, 1970. All rights reserved.

A catalogue record for this book is available from the British Library

Printed by Gutenberg Press, Tarxien, Malta

Suggestions for using *New Daylight*

Find a regular time and place, if possible, where you can read and pray undisturbed. Before you begin, take time to be still and perhaps use the BRF Prayer on page 6. Then read the Bible passage slowly (try reading it aloud if you find it over-familiar), followed by the comment. You can also use *New Daylight* for group study and discussion, if you prefer.

The prayer or point for reflection can be a starting point for your own meditation and prayer. Many people like to keep a journal to record their thoughts about a Bible passage and items for prayer. In *New Daylight* we also note the Sundays and some special festivals from the church calendar, to keep in step with the Christian year.

New Daylight and the Bible

New Daylight contributors use a range of Bible versions, and you will find a list of the versions used opposite. You are welcome to use your own preferred version alongside the passage printed in the notes. This can be particularly helpful if the Bible text has been abridged.

New Daylight affirms that the whole of the Bible is God's revelation to us, and we should read, reflect on and learn from every part of both Old and New Testaments. Usually the printed comment presents a straightforward 'thought for the day', but sometimes it may also raise questions rather than simply providing answers, as we wrestle with some of the more difficult passages of scripture.

New Daylight is also available in a deluxe edition (larger format). Visit your local Christian bookshop or BRF's online shop **brfonline.org.uk**. To obtain a cassette version for the visually impaired, contact Torch Trust for the Blind, Torch House, Torch Way, Northampton Road, Market Harborough LE16 9HL; +44 (0)1858 438260; **info@torchtrust.org**. For a Braille edition, contact St John's Guild, Sovereign House, 12–14 Warwick Street, Coventry CV5 6ET; +44 (0)24 7671 4241; **info@stjohnsguild.org**.

Comment on *New Daylight*

To send feedback, please email **enquiries@brf.org.uk**, phone **+44 (0)1865 319700** or write to the address shown opposite.

Writers in this issue

Amanda Bloor is archdeacon of Cleveland in the Diocese of York. She has a keen interest in the flourishing of clergy and enjoys helping people discover their individual gifts and callings.

Paul Gravelle is an Anglican priest in Auckland, New Zealand. He is a poet, writer and retreat leader and has ministered in military, urban and rural settings, supporting himself as an industrial journalist.

Geoff Lowson is a retired priest living in a small village in the west of County Durham. In addition to parochial ministry he spent 21 years working for the mission agency USPG.

Barbara Mosse is a writer and retired priest with experience in prison, university, hospital and mental-health chaplaincies. She has led retreats and quiet days and has lectured in theological education. Her books include *Encircling the Christian Year* and *Welcoming the Way of the Cross* (both BRF).

David Runcorn is a 'free-range priest' involved with ministry training, teaching, support and spiritual direction. His books include *The Gift of Tears* (Canterbury, 2018) and *Love Means Love* (SPCK, 2020). **davidruncorn.com**.

Elizabeth Rundle has written many study and devotional books. She has written and presented scripts for local and national radio and television and organised and led 16 pilgrimages to the Holy Land. A retired Methodist minister, Elizabeth served churches in Cornwall and London.

Jane Walters (Jane Clamp) is the author of *Too Soon: A mother's journey through miscarriage* (SPCK, 2018) and a speaker at Christian events. She runs writing groups in her local rural Norfolk as well as Christian creative writing retreats further afield. **janeclamp.com**.

Rosie Ward is a retired priest who now divides her time between her local parish and her other interests, including the environment, vocation and women's ministry. She has written several books and booklets, including *Growing Women Leaders* (BRF/CPAS, 2008).

Veronica Zundel is an Oxford graduate, writer and columnist. She lives with her husband and son in north London. Her most recent book is *Everything I Know about God, I've Learned from Being a Parent* (BRF, 2013).

Sally Welch writes…

One of the challenges of writing the introduction for these reflections is that I have to do so a full year before you read it. Sometimes this works incredibly well – when the March 2020 lockdown for coronavirus was in place, we were studying the book of Ezekiel, which has some wise words for those facing challenging circumstances. However, on other occasions it is perhaps not so helpful – as I write this, we are still in lockdown; we do not know the future course of the pandemic, and the world trembles. Therefore, I must step outside my immediate circumstances in order to address future readers in whatever situation you are in.

Fortunately, as I write I can see our five chickens scratching around on the lawn, helpfully raking the moss as they search for insects. When lost for inspiration, I can watch the birds on the feeder in front of the study window and marvel at the clouds of blossom that float across my view as the wind shakes the flowering cherry just out of sight. As the author of Genesis reminds us, we live in God's promise that 'as long as the earth endures, seedtime and harvest, cold and heat, summer and winter, day and night, shall not cease' (Genesis 8:22, NRSV). The rainbow has been adopted as a sign of hope for the future – let us be keepers of that hope, surrounded by the reassurances of creation.

Late spring and summer is a good time to explore some of the more challenging aspects of life and faith; surrounded by signs of God's care for us, we have a reassuring context in which to reflect and pray. So Amanda Bloor will help us to examine the biblical concept of judgement, while Rosie Ward looks at the second book of Kings in a Christian context. David Runcorn leads us through some reflections on ageing, while Jane Walters encourages us to think about the nature of church and Christian life as revealed in the letters of Paul to Timothy. We also continue our exploration of Holy Habits by looking at worship, with Paul Gravelle – who partners us from New Zealand – offering an interesting view on things from over there.

As I rejoice in the signs of spring which surround me, I send my prayers forward to you all, that you too may rejoice in the signs of God's love for each one of us, wherever they are to be found.

Sally Ann Welch

The BRF Prayer

Almighty God,
you have taught us that your word is a lamp for our feet
and a light for our path. Help us, and all who prayerfully
read your word, to deepen our fellowship with you
and with each other through your love.
And in so doing may we come to know you more fully,
love you more truly, and follow more faithfully
in the steps of your Son Jesus Christ, who lives and reigns
with you and the Holy Spirit, one God forevermore.
Amen

Were you there? BRF celebrates its centenary in 2022 and we'd love you to share your BRF memories with us. We've already heard from supporters with wonderful stories. Beryl Fudge attended our 25th anniversary service in Westminster Central Hall in 1947, in the presence of the Queen Mother and Princess Margaret. Catharine Heron was prepared for confirmation in 1945 by our founder, Canon Leslie Mannering, and still has his duplicated notes in their original brown cardboard folder.

Do you have a BRF story to tell, whether of events, people, books or Bible reading notes? Please email **eley.mcainsh@brf.org.uk**, call **01865 319708** or write to **Eley McAinsh** at BRF, 15 The Chambers, Vineyard, Abingdon, OX14 3FE, United Kingdom.

Daniel

 The book of Daniel is an unusual and intriguing text. Part of its difficulty lies in the textual and literary problems that have baffled generations of scholars. This aside, for the reader approaching this book as we do, as a basis for daily prayer and reflection, there is much here to invite and challenge, stimulate and provoke. Here are the familiar Sunday-school stories of Daniel in the lions' den and Shadrach, Meshach and Abednego in the fiery furnace. Here too is the terror of the writing on the wall at Belshazzar's feast, and the constant danger faced by Daniel and his countrymen as they bravely claim their belief and trust in the God of Israel in an alien land.

The book is divided into two distinct parts: chapters 1—6 offer a variety of tales from the royal court of Babylon, and chapters 7—12 detail a series of apocalyptic (a Greek word relating to revelation) visions and their interpretation. Although the book's precise date is unclear, the background to both parts concerns Judah's experience of military defeat, oppression and exile in a foreign land: chapters 1—6 relate to the deportation to Babylon, and chapters 7—12 to a visionary take on the nation's oppression under various foreign rulers, culminating with the reign of the Greek king Antiochus IV Epiphanes.

The order of our reflections here follows the sequence of the book, and we first accompany Daniel and his friends through their arrival at the royal court of Nebuchadnezzar and the dramatic things that happen to them there as they uphold their own faith in a foreign land (reflections 1–8). The second section, with its apocalyptic, visionary language and concern with the end times, is considered in reflections 9—15. The narrative sequences of these stories and visions are lengthy and are necessarily presented here in an abridged form; a reading of the entire relevant episode is strongly recommended.

As with all biblical material, the world we enter here is one that is strange to us and many centuries removed in time. But though times and circumstances may change, human nature, with its strengths and weaknesses, its quirks and foibles, seems to alter very little. We will encounter much in these texts that encourages reflection on issues relevant to our time.

BARBARA MOSSE

A subject people

In the third year of the reign of King Jehoiakim of Judah, King Nebuchad-nezzar of Babylon came to Jerusalem and besieged it. The Lord let King Jehoiakim of Judah fall into his power, as well as some of the vessels of the house of God. These he... placed... in the treasury of his gods. Then the king commanded his palace master Ashpenaz to bring some of the Israelites of the royal family and of the nobility, young men without physi-cal defect and handsome, versed in every branch of wisdom, endowed with knowledge and insight, and competent to serve in the king's palace; they were to be taught the literature and language of the Chaldeans. The king assigned them a daily portion... of food and wine... Among them were Daniel, Hananiah, Mishael and Azariah, from the tribe of Judah.

The opening two verses of Daniel set the context for the entire book. Disas-ter has struck: Jerusalem has been besieged and taken by Nebuchadnezzar king of Babylon. The powerlessness of the conquered nation is underlined by Nebuchadnezzar's stealing of Judah's holy vessels and their placement in the treasury of the Babylonian gods.

On to this stage step Daniel and his three compatriots, chosen to serve at Nebuchadnezzar's court. There is a suggestion of the idea of sacrifice here: the chosen men are to be 'without physical defect and handsome', as well as being endowed with precocious intellectual giftedness. They are to be educated in the ways of the Babylonians and fed with 'royal rations' of food and wine.

For the contemporary reader, one of the greatest challenges in this passage perhaps lies in the statement that 'the Lord let King Jehoiakim of Judah fall into [Nebuchadnezzar's] power'. We will hopefully resist the temptation to make crude associations between cataclysmic events and God's judgement – and yet the challenge remains. We readily see and appreciate God's hand at work in the positive and joyous events of life; but how do we react when things go badly wrong, whether on a personal or national level? Are we able to acknowledge the loving hand of God at work in *all* the circumstances of our lives?

'We know that all things work together for good for those who love God,
who are called according to his purpose' (Romans 8:28).

Resistance through food

But Daniel resolved that he would not defile himself with the royal rations of food and wine... The palace master said to Daniel, 'I am afraid of my lord the king; he has appointed your food and drink...' Then Daniel asked the guard whom the palace master had appointed over Daniel, Hananiah, Mishael and Azariah: 'Please test your servants for ten days. Let us be given vegetables to eat and water to drink. You can then compare our appearance with the appearance of the young men who eat the royal rations, and deal with your servants according to what you observe'... At the end of ten days it was observed that they appeared better and fatter than all the young men who had been eating the royal rations.

The primary function of food has always been to sustain our bodies. But food as a commodity has also functioned as a potent source of protest, from highchair-bound toddlers, driving their parents to despair through their refusal to eat, to hunger strikers, seeking to draw attention to their cause.

In today's reading, Daniel and his friends, as part of their preparation for life in the royal court, have been allocated royal rations of food and wine. This offends their religious sensibilities, and they seek permission to restrict their diet to vegetables alone. In taking this stance, they not only affirm their adherence to their God (as against the gods of the Babylonians), but also wrest back one tiny area of control that has been taken from them by the occupying force.

Dieting may be one way we seek to keep control of our body weight, and we may make decisions about food on a wider canvas, by choosing to shop and eat more sustainably in the light of the growing reality of global warming. We may offer our own resistance in seeking a more sustainable way of living than that encouraged in mainstream society.

In what ways do we resist the attempts of the consumerist perspective to assimilate us more deeply into its vision and outlook? And do we see this resistance as part of our response to the call of God in our lives?

BARBARA MOSSE

Resistance vindicated

So the guard continued to withdraw their royal rations and the wine they were to drink, and gave them vegetables. To these four young men God gave knowledge and skill in every aspect of literature and wisdom; Daniel also had insight into all visions and dreams. At the end of the time that the king had set for them to be brought in, the palace master brought them into the presence of Nebuchadnezzar, and the king spoke with them. And among them all, no one was found to compare with Daniel, Hananiah, Mishael and Azariah; therefore they were stationed in the king's court.

At the end of their ten-day trial eating only vegetables, not only were Daniel and his friends healthier than the other young men being trained for the king's court, but they also continued to exhibit precocious wisdom. This vindication wasn't, however, the main motivation for Daniel and his friends; their concern was simply to remain faithful to God in their restricted circumstances.

Yesterday we considered some of the ways in which we could learn, like Daniel, to seek the wisdom that would enable us to ask deeper questions of the culture and time in which we find ourselves. A powerful example from relatively recent times is offered in the stance taken by the 18th-century American Quaker minister John Woolman, who refused to wear any items of clothing that had been made – or dyed – with slave labour. In our own day, almost three centuries later, with the continuing existence of sweat shops and the proliferation of cheap, throwaway clothing, the challenge is still a live one. But if we rise to it, we may well, unlike Daniel, attract criticism rather than praise from the society in which we live.

'God appeared to Solomon, and said to him, "Ask what I should give you."
Solomon said to God, "You have shown great and steadfast love to my
father David, and have made me succeed him as king… Give me now
wisdom and knowledge to go out and come in"' (2 Chronicles 1:7–10,
abridged). Solomon could have asked for many other things: possessions,
wealth, honour, vengeance on his enemies, long life. Are we able to make
his prayer our own?

BARBARA MOSSE

An impossible command

In the second year of Nebuchadnezzar's reign, Nebuchadnezzar dreamed such dreams that his spirit was troubled and his sleep left him. So the king commanded that the magicians, the enchanters, the sorcerers and the Chaldeans be summoned to tell the king his dreams… The Chaldeans said to the king (in Aramaic), 'O king, live forever! Tell your servants the dream, and we will reveal the interpretation.' The king answered the Chaldeans, 'This is a public decree: if you do not tell me both the dream and its interpretation, you shall be torn limb from limb, and your houses shall be laid in ruins. But if you do tell me the dream and the interpretation, you shall receive from me gifts and rewards and great honour.'

Here we see Nebuchadnezzar at his most petulant. Troubled by his dreams, the demand that his magicians tell him both the dream and its interpretation is totally unreasonable and impossible to fulfil. It is perhaps unlikely that we will ever find ourselves in a situation quite as drastic as this, with a life-or-death demand no human ingenuity can satisfy. We may, however, sometimes find ourselves in situations for which there is no easy or obvious answer; dilemmas where there is no clear right or wrong choice. The gospels portray Jesus encountering a number of such situations, usually being posed questions by his opponents when they are trying to trap him.

John 8:2–11 is a passage familiar to many. Here the scribes and Pharisees try to trap Jesus into condemning a woman caught in adultery to be stoned to death – in accordance with Mosaic law – or setting her free in defiance of that law. Jesus' response, after a time of reflection when he writes with his finger on the ground, is, 'Let anyone among you who is without sin be the first to throw a stone at her' (John 8:7). And his opponents go away discomforted.

When we are put on the spot, we may find ourselves, like Jesus and the magicians in Daniel, under pressure from other people's agendas and motivations. The magicians were thrown into panic; but Jesus refused to be hurried.

In seemingly impossible situations, are we able to reflect and give space for a possible 'third way' solution to emerge?

BARBARA MOSSE

Credit where credit is due

The mystery was revealed to Daniel in a vision of the night, and Daniel blessed the God of heaven… Therefore Daniel went to Arioch, whom the king had appointed to destroy the wise men of Babylon, and said to him, 'Do not destroy the wise men of Babylon; bring me in before the king, and I will give the king the interpretation'… The king said to Daniel, whose name was Belteshazzar, 'Are you able to tell me the dream that I have seen and its interpretation?' Daniel answered the king, 'No wise men, enchanters, magicians or diviners can show the king the mystery that the king is asking, but there is a God in heaven who reveals mysteries, and he has disclosed to King Nebuchadnezzar what will happen at the end of days.'

The problem Nebuchadnezzar has posed his wise men seems to have no solution – until God reveals the answer to Daniel in 'a vision of the night'. Daniel's immediate request to Arioch to be taken to the king displays immense courage. To stand before the king is to place himself in a situation of danger, threat and total unpredictability. A king who makes the outrageous and capricious demands that Nebuchadnezzar has made of his wise men can't be trusted to act rationally or reasonably, and Daniel knows that his message is not one the king wants to hear. But Daniel's trust in God is greater than his fear of Nebuchadnezzar.

Our passage begins with Daniel fully aware of the divine source of his knowledge. Without this certainty of God's intervention, he would have been in no better position than the king's other wise men and magicians. It is significant that Daniel's opening response to the king's demand affirms that God, and God alone, is the source of the interpretation of the king's dream; any ingenuity on Daniel's part doesn't come into it.

The situation in which Daniel finds himself here is fraught with danger, and is one that, hopefully, few of us will experience. But we may experience many circumstances when we are given the right words to say or action to perform. Are we able (and willing) at those times to resist the temptation to bask in people's praise – and to give God the glory?

BARBARA MOSSE

But if not...

'There are certain Jews... Shadrach, Meshach and Abednego. These pay no heed to you, O king. They do not serve your gods and they do not worship the golden statue that you have set up.' Then Nebuchadnezzar in furious rage... said to them... 'If you do not worship, you shall immediately be thrown into a furnace of blazing fire, and who is the god who will deliver you out of my hands?' [They] answered the king, 'O Nebuchadnezzar, we have no need to present a defence to you in this matter. If our God... is able to deliver us... let him deliver us. But if not... we will not serve your gods and we will not worship the golden statue that you have set up.'

David Watson was a world-famous priest, evangelist and leading figure in the charismatic renewal movement. He died in 1984 of cancer, at the age of 51. His final book was *Fear No Evil*, in which he shared his doubts and anxieties, but also his firm faith in God in the face of his approaching death. When he did die, many of his followers were shaken to their roots. How could God allow such a thing to happen? They had been convinced he would be healed. For these Christians, there had to be a reason. I remember feeling quite disturbed when the 'reason' many people settled on was that David Watson was being punished for his grandmother's sin in reading tea leaves!

In today's passage, the reason for the threat facing Daniel's three friends is clear. They have been set up by their enemies and have fallen foul of the royal decree that all should pray to the king's golden statue. They refuse to submit, even with the threat of being thrown into the furnace. Their response is challenging: God may deliver them, and if so, all well and good; but if not – it will make no difference to their decision. It takes a special courage to accept what comes in faith – even if it is not the outcome we would wish for.

'Yea, though I walk through the valley of the shadow of death, I will fear no evil: for thou art with me; thy rod and thy staff they comfort me'
(Psalm 23:4, KJV).

BARBARA MOSSE

Weighed on the scales

King Belshazzar made a great festival for a thousand of his lords, and he was drinking wine in the presence of the thousand… They drank the wine and praised the gods of gold and silver, bronze, iron, wood and stone. Immediately the fingers of a human hand appeared and began writing on the… wall of the royal palace… Then the king's face turned pale, and his thoughts terrified him… [Daniel said,] 'The God in whose power is your very breath… you have not honoured. So from his presence the hand was sent… This is the interpretation… MENE, God has numbered the days of your kingdom and brought it to an end; TEKEL, you have been weighed on the scales and found wanting; PERES, your kingdom is divided and given to the Medes and the Persians'… That very night Belshazzar… was killed.

The theologian Daniel L. Smith-Christopher asks, 'What was the nature of the "sin" of Belshazzar?' (*New Interpreter's Bible*, vol. VII, p. 84). In relation to today's narrative he focuses on the details of Belshazzar's banquet, including the desecration of the temple vessels. There is an ongoing theme here of the abuse of a conquered people: a trampling underfoot of cherished culture and values, ritual humiliation and an attempted destruction of faith identity. Smith-Christopher writes of the evidence of 'the most insidious elements of imperial power and oppression'. As an American, he finds echoes of these tendencies within his own country's history, such as the desecration of native American holy sites by Captain James Cook and the massacre of the Cheyenne and Arapaho people at Sand Creek in 1864. Looking at the question through our own eyes, we may well be able to add examples from our own nation's perspective and historical experience.

But the questions raised here don't just apply to nations; there is relevance for the individual too. These issues lead me to ask uncomfortable personal questions. Have there been times in my life when I have found myself gloating over someone else's failure? Have I ever been in a situation where I thought myself superior? Have I ever been disrespectful or dismissive of other people's cherished beliefs?

How many times have I 'been weighed on the scales and found wanting'?

BARBARA MOSSE

True faithfulness

Although Daniel knew that the document had been signed, he continued… to get down on his knees three times a day to pray to his God and praise him, just as he had done previously. The conspirators… approached the king and said… 'Daniel… pays no attention to you… but he is saying his prayers three times a day.' When the king heard the charge, he was very much distressed… Then the conspirators came to the king and said… 'Know, O king, that it is a law of the Medes and the Persians that no interdict or ordinance that the king establishes can be changed.' Then… Daniel was… thrown into the den of lions… Then, at break of day, the king got up and hurried to the den of lions… Daniel then said to the king, 'O king, live forever! My God sent his angels and shut the lions' mouths so that they would not hurt me.'

The severe testing of his three friends in the fiery furnace through the malice of the king's advisors now lands directly at Daniel's door. Darius is an unwise king who has stupidly let the conspirators trap him in a corner, and when they tell the king that Daniel continues to pray to his God three times a day in defiance of Darius' order, the king has no choice but to act.

A question I haven't heard recently, but which was very much around two or three decades ago, was, 'If you were arrested and brought to trial on a charge of being a Christian, would there be enough evidence to convict you?' In those days I didn't really consider that the question was one I could usefully ask of myself, and assumed that it would only really be relevant in countries where Christianity was a persecuted religion. How wrong I was! In a culture where the Christian faith is no longer centre stage and, in many cases, treated as an irrelevance, the temptation perhaps has a slightly different emphasis. Do I try to fit in too much with the prevailing culture? What difference, if any, does my Christianity make – to my attitudes, behaviour and relationships?

'For those who want to save their life will lose it… Those who are ashamed of me and of my words, of them the Son of Man will be ashamed when he comes in his glory' (Luke 9:24, 26).

BARBARA MOSSE

On the ground of your great mercies

In the first year of Darius… I, Daniel, perceived in the books the number of years that, according to the word of the Lord to the prophet Jeremiah, must be fulfilled for the devastation of Jerusalem, namely, seventy years. Then I turned to the Lord God, to seek an answer by prayer and supplication with fasting and sackcloth and ashes. I prayed to the Lord my God and made confession, saying… 'O Lord… let your anger and wrath… turn away from your city Jerusalem, your holy mountain; because of our sins and the iniquities of our ancestors, Jerusalem and your people have become a disgrace… We do not present our supplication before you on the ground of our righteousness, but on the ground of your great mercies.'

Daniel is listed in scripture among the minor prophets, but unusually he is never recorded as addressing the people with the words of God. Daniel's prayer of confession here and his identification with his people's disgrace do, however, resonate with the experience of other prophets (see, for example, Jeremiah 8:18–22). Most significantly, his words anticipate the actions of Jesus, who also expressed deep concern for the state of Jerusalem, weeping over its inability to recognise 'the things that make for peace' (Luke 19:42).

Prophets were fallible human beings like their people, and they were able, as Daniel does here, to identify with the people's disgrace in making their confession. But Jesus was the Son of God and sinless, and, in his voluntary embracing of the cross, he was able to make that identification complete – 'a full, perfect and sufficient sacrifice… for the sins of the whole world' (*Book of Common Prayer*, 1549).

We may receive a sign of the cross in ash on our forehead on Ash Wednesday, but apart from this yearly act, visible demonstrations of repentance among us are rare. We tend to recoil from the thought that we are 'miserable sinners'. But perhaps what we really lack is humility, which is less about beating ourselves up and more to do with a realistic acceptance of our littleness in relation to God.

'We are not worthy so much as to gather up the crumbs under your table. But you are the same Lord, whose nature is always to have mercy' (*'Prayer of humble access', Book of Common Prayer*).

BARBARA MOSSE

Desolations are decreed

While I was speaking, and was praying and confessing my sin and the sin of my people Israel… while I was speaking in prayer, the man Gabriel, whom I had seen before in a vision, came to me in swift flight at the time of the evening sacrifice. He came and said to me, 'Daniel, I have now come out to give you wisdom and understanding… So consider the word and understand the vision: Seventy weeks are decreed for your people and your holy city: to finish the transgression, to put an end to sin, and to atone… to bring in everlasting righteousness… Know therefore and understand… Its end shall come with a flood, and to the end there shall be war. Desolations are decreed.'

I am writing these reflections on the book of Daniel in the middle of the coronavirus pandemic, with as yet no end in sight. Gabriel's message offers a glimmer of hope to Daniel in his situation, as he reassures him that there will be an end to Israel's troubles. But before that resolution times will be harsh – 'desolations are decreed'. Things will get a lot worse before they get better.

This message to Daniel is important, because however rational our minds may be, we can find we struggle spiritually when life gets difficult. Where is God in all this? There is an amusing story – probably apocryphal – concerning the 16th-century Spanish saint and mystic Teresa of Ávila. While riding her horse one day, she fell off and landed in a patch of mud. At this point she heard Jesus say to her, 'This is how I treat my friends.' 'Lord,' she replied, 'if this is how you treat your friends, it's no wonder that you have so few of them!'

Today's passage encourages us to hang on in faith, however difficult or painful our circumstances, and not to simply hang on, but to seek within our difficulties the depths of trust that will enable us – as the apostle Paul later urged – to 'give thanks in all circumstances' (1 Thessalonians 5:18).

'The more our senses are faithless, revolted, uncertain and in despair,
the more surely faith says, "This is God; all is well"'
(Jean-Pierre de Caussade, 1675–1751).

BARBARA MOSSE

You are safe

On the twenty-fourth day of the first month, as I was standing on the bank of the great river (that is, the Tigris), I looked up and saw a man clothed in linen, with a belt of gold from Uphaz around his waist… He said to me, 'Daniel, greatly beloved, pay attention to the words that I am going to speak to you. Stand on your feet, for I have now been sent to you.' So… I stood up trembling. He said to me, 'Do not fear, Daniel, for from the first day that you set your mind to gain understanding and to humble yourself before your God, your words have been heard… Greatly beloved, you are safe. Be strong and courageous!' When he spoke to me, I was strengthened and said, 'Let my lord speak, for you have strengthened me.'

Daniel the visionary is the main focus of this second half of the book, just as the exploits of Daniel and his compatriots at the Babylonian court were the chief concern of the earlier chapters. But the division is to some extent a false one, as the whole book relates to the contrast between the reign of God and that of earthly rulers. Today's passage is significant in that the vision involves a messenger who speaks to Daniel; previously, Daniel has simply watched the vision. The words of 'the man', who is clearly a divine messenger, are reminiscent of those of the Lord to Joshua on the eve of battle (Joshua 1:1–9) and were similarly intended to inspire, encourage and strengthen.

   We too may gain encouragement here. But it is important that we do not overlook what precedes this encouragement. Daniel has 'set [his] mind to gain understanding and to humble [himself] before [his] God' (v. 12). The challenge to each one of us is to remain open to the loving action of God in humility, trust and perseverance, whether the times are good or bad, turbulent or untroubled. Then – perhaps in defiance of the times through which we are living – we will know ourselves to be beloved and safe.

'Be strong and courageous; do not be frightened or dismayed,
for the Lord your God is with you wherever you go' (Joshua 1:9).

BARBARA MOSSE

It shall not succeed

'Then shall arise… one who shall send an official for the glory of the kingdom; but within a few days he shall be broken, though not in anger or in battle. In his place shall arise a contemptible person on whom royal majesty had not been conferred; he shall come in without warning and obtain the kingdom through intrigue… He shall stir up his power and determination against the king of the south with a great army, and the king of the south shall wage war with a much greater and stronger army… The two kings, their minds bent on evil, shall sit at one table and exchange lies. But it shall not succeed, for there remains an end at the time appointed.'

As a result of the words of the heavenly messenger, Daniel finds he can speak with prophetic insight – and the picture he paints is bleak. He speaks of a future time when one working for the good of the kingdom 'shall be broken', and in whose place shall come 'a contemptible person', who gains the kingdom deviously rather than through legitimately conferred authority. Law and order will have broken down, kings will have 'their minds bent on evil' and war, inevitably, will be the result. There may be uncomfortable resonances here for us as we consider our own world and its current problems.

However, just when it appears that there is no hope to be had anywhere, Daniel adds a vitally important – and unexpected – 'but'. With that little word, Daniel gathers up all the death, devastation and disaster foreseen in his earlier words and calmly states, 'It shall not succeed.' And the reason? 'There remains an end at the time appointed.'

Despite all physical evidence to the contrary, God remains in control and will bring the time of trouble to an end. This is no flighty pie-in-the-sky-when-you-die message. As well as encouragement, Daniel's words offer a challenge to his readers' faith in tough times – how do *you* react when your world collapses?

'Because you have made the Lord your refuge, the Most High your dwelling-place, no evil shall befall you, no scourge come near your tent. For he will command his angels concerning you to guard you in all your ways'
(Psalm 91:9–11).

BARBARA MOSSE

He shall exalt himself

'The king shall act as he pleases. He shall exalt himself and consider himself greater than any god, and shall speak horrendous things against the God of gods. He shall prosper until the period of wrath is completed, for what is determined shall be done. He shall pay no respect to the gods of his ancestors, or to the one beloved by women; he shall pay no respect to any other god, for he shall consider himself greater than all. He shall honour the god of fortresses… He shall deal with the strongest fortresses by the help of a foreign god. Those who acknowledge him he shall make more wealthy, and shall appoint them as rulers over many, and shall distribute the land for a price.'

The call to leadership is a serious responsibility, and this thinly veiled attack on the pagan ruler Antiochus IV could be seen as a description of how *not* to go about it. Antiochus was a Greek who ruled the Israelites between 175 and 164 BC, who persecuted those in Judea and Samaria and who tried to enforce Greek culture on all the peoples of his kingdom. He believed he was invincible, claiming for himself the title 'God manifest' (Epiphanes).

It may not be difficult to recognise elements of these characteristics, with their total lack of humility, in some individuals in local, national or international public life today. What may be harder, however, is recognising those same characteristics when they are uncomfortably closer to home. Have I ever been so sure of my own authority and rightness that I saw no need to seek the advice of those to whom I was accountable? I trust that I have never spoken 'horrendous things against the God of gods', but have I ever left God out of the reckoning and simply did my own thing? How have the decisions I have made and the actions I have taken affected the lives of others, for good or evil?

'Jesus, knowing that the Father had given all things into his hands, and that he had come from God and was going to God… poured water into a basin and began to wash the disciples' feet and to wipe them with the towel that was tied around him' (John 13:3, 5).

BARBARA MOSSE

Keep the words secret

'At that time Michael, the great prince, the protector of your people, shall arise. There shall be a time of anguish, such as has never occurred since nations came into existence. But at that time your people shall be delivered, everyone who is found written in the book. Many of those who sleep in the dust of the earth shall awake, some to everlasting life, and some to shame and everlasting contempt. Those who are wise shall shine like the brightness of the sky, and those who lead many to righteousness, like the stars forever and ever. But you, Daniel, keep the words secret and the book sealed until the time of the end. Many shall be running back and forth, and evil shall increase.'

As the book of Daniel draws to a close, the archangel Michael, the protector of the Israelite people, reappears (see Daniel 10:13). His presence here is because there is to be a time of great anguish that will lead to Israel's deliverance, and Michael is seen as a comforting and protecting presence.

And then there is the mysterious injunction to Daniel to 'keep the words secret and the book sealed until the end of time'. There is some anticipation here of the 'Messianic secret' of Mark's gospel, where people whom Jesus has healed are then ordered not to tell anyone about it (such as in Mark 7:36).

There is an idea here that the things that really matter take time and reflection to come to full fruition, and too much early exposure can be fatal. We live in a society where reticence is not encouraged; people's thoughts and feelings are splashed all over social media with little or no reflection or consideration. As a society, the idea of 'biding our time' doesn't come easily to us, and we can be tempted to talk too much too soon about what we don't fully understand. But our journey with God unfolds over a lifetime, and the quality of waiting is one we need as we put our roots down deeper into the soil of faith.

'For everything there is a season, and a time for every matter under heaven: a time to be born, and a time to die... a time to keep silence, and a time to speak' (Ecclesiastes 3:1–2, 7).

BARBARA MOSSE

Go your way, and rest

The man clothed in linen… raised his right hand and his left hand towards heaven. And I heard him swear by the one who lives forever that it would be for a time, two times, and half a time, and that when the shattering of the power of the holy people comes to an end, all these things would be accomplished. I heard but could not understand; so I said, 'My lord, what shall be the outcome of these things?' He said, 'Go your way, Daniel, for the words are to remain secret and sealed until the time of the end. Many shall be purified, cleansed and refined, but the wicked shall continue to act wickedly. None of the wicked shall understand, but those who are wise shall understand… Happy are those who persevere… But you, go your way, and rest; you shall rise for your reward at the end of the days.'

It has been a strange and awesome experience, working on these reflections as the coronavirus has been ravaging our nation and our world. There have been several unsettling resonances and parallels between Daniel's world and our own. The reference to 'the shattering of the power of the holy people' connects challengingly with the church, whose doors are, for now, shut against priests and people, and which is having to find fresh and innovative ways to reach out with the gospel and to keep its people connected in these unprecedented times. Our 'enemy' may have been an invisible virus rather than an invading army, but it has taken us hostage and enforced an entirely new pattern of living on us just as powerfully and effectively as the Babylonian invasion did for the Israelites.

We, like Daniel, ask the question, 'What shall be the outcome of these things?' And, like Daniel, as yet we have no complete answer. But there is reassurance, both then and now. Anticipating the words of Jesus in the 'little apocalypse' of Mark – 'But the one who endures to the end will be saved' (Mark 13:13) – Daniel is told, 'Happy are those who persevere… go your way, and rest.'

'For God alone my soul waits in silence; from him comes my salvation. He alone is my rock and my salvation, my fortress; I shall never be shaken' (Psalm 62:1–2).

BARBARA MOSSE

Worship (a holy habit)

Worship can have a very broad meaning at times, and at others a much more specific one. Brother Lawrence, whose *The Practice of the Presence of God* has inspired so many, saw worship as including everything he did, while my dictionary defines worship simply as 'homage or reverence paid to a deity'. When we talk about places of worship or worship songs, we are striking new meanings somewhere in between.

Perhaps we feel that worship is what we do in church. But is everything we do in church really worship? Or should it be? One problem with these different interpretations is that it is possible to miss out altogether on the sort of worship that our God tells us he really wants.

I have recently been trying to give closer attention to the songs and hymns that I sing in church. I find that those which best help me to worship are those which are addressed directly to God. A lot of what we say and sing is about God, but it seems to me that it is only by praising, reverencing and paying homage to God directly, either together or individually, that we are really beginning to get to the true meaning of worship. What do you think? We will see that Jesus taught his disciples something about this.

It will be profitable for us to look at this topic together because some of us (including me) may have overemphasised different aspects of worship, either alone or when we are together in church. Some of us will be very upfront with the praise and thanksgiving aspects of our approach to God. If we are that way inclined, might it be that the reverence and homage need to receive a little more emphasis?

In the first week, we will reflect on the wider meanings of worship. In the second week, however, we will look at worship in a more specific way. Let's see if we can discover some aspect of worship that is new for us. I recall being told, and have certainly found it to be true, that it is a source of great joy when we are able to discover something new about our God.

PAUL GRAVELLE

Worship then and now (1)

Adam and his wife had another son. She said, 'God has given me a son to replace Abel, whom Cain killed.' So she named him Seth. Seth had a son whom he named Enosh. It was then that people began using the Lord's holy name in worship.

Is this the beginning of corporate worship – the first mention of people gathering together with the intent and purpose of acknowledging and praising God? There would have been quite a lot of people around by this time, enough to make up a significant congregation. The verses immediately before this tell us that Cain's descendants seemed to be following in their father's footsteps. Lamech, Cain's great-great-grandson, killed a young man who had struck him. 'Seventy-seven lives will be taken,' he claimed, 'if anyone kills me.' Was this Cain's nature that had been passed down or simply a behavioural pattern passed from father to son?

Here, however, was another branch of the family that seemed determined to follow a different and better way. Right from those early days of the human story, meeting together to worship the Lord was seen by some as a better alternative to giving in to the natural instinct for doing evil. The descendants of Cain were seen as the perpetrators of evil, but the descendants of Abel's replacement in the family are portrayed as making a right and better choice.

God has given his human creation the ability to choose between right and wrong. When a group of people decide to 'use the Lord's holy name in worship' together, they at once become an effective force against evil in the world. And this is how the Bible describes the church. *The Message* puts Jesus' own words on this subject in a graphic and memorable way: 'This is the rock on which I will put together my church, a church so expansive with energy that not even the gates of hell will be able to keep it out' (Matthew 16:18).

In what ways are you and those in your church succeeding in breaking down the gates of hell in the way you worship? What could be done to increase your effectiveness in this?

PAUL GRAVELLE

Worship then and now (2)

The first covenant had rules for worship… The priests go into the outer tent every day to perform their duties, but only the high priest goes into the inner tent, and he does so only once a year. He takes with him blood which he offers to God on behalf of himself and for the sins which the people have committed without knowing they were sinning… How much more is accomplished by the blood of Christ!… His blood will purify our consciences from useless rituals.

Once the Israelites had escaped from slavery in Egypt, a complex code of rules for worship was laid down. We find these rules in the books of Exodus and Leviticus. The letter to the Hebrews was addressed to Jewish converts who were steeped in these rules. But the rules and rituals laid down by Moses were now made redundant by the once-and-for-all sacrifice made by Jesus on the cross. These Jews needed a clear explanation of the relationship between the old form of worship and the new. The common factor between old and new was that blood must be shed and life sacrificed if sins were to be forgiven; the huge difference was that both the daily and the special yearly sacrifices were now entirely unnecessary.

For these early Jewish converts, the same awe and reverence for God applied, just as it does for us today. But we now enjoy something that was barely realised in Old Testament times – the intense love of God, which we see particularly in Jesus.

Worship has changed dramatically since Jesus came among us and then sent his loving Spirit to fill us. Many have found new dimensions of worship since watching *The Shack*, a film in which the persons of the Trinity are depicted as three very human, yet essentially divine, characters. At the same time, as Hebrews later reminds us, God has never relinquished that same awesome, all-powerful, fiery presence that he demonstrates in the Old Testament. We should never forget this, whether we find worship a little tedious and boring or if it becomes wildly exciting and exuberant.

---

*'Let us be grateful and worship God in a way that will please him, with reverence and awe, because our God is indeed a destroying fire'
(Hebrews 12:28–29).*

PAUL GRAVELLE

'Worship no god but me'

Elijah answered… 'You are disobeying the Lord's commands and worshipping the idols of Baal…' So Ahab summoned all the Israelites and the prophets of Baal to meet at Mount Carmel. Elijah went up to the people and said, 'How much longer will it take you to make up your minds? If the Lord is God, worship him; but if Baal is God, worship him!' But the people didn't say a word.

Elijah accused the people of breaking the very first of the ten commandments: 'Worship no god but me' (Exodus 20:3). We who use *New Daylight* and read our Bibles religiously every day are never in danger of doing that! Or are we?

I can think of more than one occasion when, perhaps after going to bed later than usual on a Saturday and oversleeping a bit in the morning, I have said, 'I think I'll give church a miss today.' My 'other god' was my own lazy body!

If I had gone to church, I would have been confronted with those words of Jesus that are his interpretation of that first commandment: 'Love the Lord your God with all your heart, with all your soul, with all your mind and with all your strength' (Mark 12:30). Those words always bring me up short. How can anyone hope to keep a commandment like that?

Are we, then, faced with an impossible choice: if we choose to worship God, rather than our own inclinations, we find ourselves confronted by a God whose commands are impossible to keep? This is where we discover that worship, like every kind of communion with our God, is a two-way process, because confession of our failures is also a part of our worship. God's forgiveness, because of what he has done through Jesus, is his ready response.

And have you considered that there might be a way of worshipping God that really pleases him? We shall be looking into this shortly – watch this space.

Are you able to let yourself really feel God's forgiveness after you have confessed your failures to him? In what other ways might you expect to feel God's response and pleasure when you worship him?

PAUL GRAVELLE

Where worship begins

When King Solomon finished his prayer, fire came down from heaven and burned up the sacrifices that had been offered, and the dazzling light of the Lord's presence filled the Temple. Because the Temple was full of the dazzling light, the priests could not enter it. When the people of Israel saw the fire fall from heaven and the light fill the Temple, they fell face downward on the pavement, worshipping God.

I have just an inkling of what happened to the people at the dedication of Solomon's temple. In December 2018, I was visiting Christchurch's 'Cardboard Cathedral' – a provisional building erected after the disastrous earthquake of 2010. It was a weekday. No service was in progress. The nave was buzzing with tourists. A small cherry-picker was putting a Christmas tree together. Suddenly, my wife and I were totally overcome by the presence of God. We couldn't speak. We had to sit down on the nearest seat until our strength returned. God himself was right there, amid all that was going on around us. Every time I see the interior of the cathedral on TV, look at the photograph we purchased at the time or even simply recall that moment, the same vital sensation of the immediate presence of God returns.

I expect some of you may have had a similar experience. But, while these may seem like one-offs, they are given to us as reminders of Jesus' assurance that he is always with us, 'to the end of the age', no matter what else may be going on.

This is where worship really begins, doesn't it? It begins at the point where, no matter what else has been going on for us or how we feel about it, we recognise who we are approaching and in whose awe-inspiring, yet loving and compassionate, presence we are. Do you find it easier to worship in this way when you are gathered with others or when you are on your own? As we shall see, God has a real desire for us to worship him.

Close your eyes now and try to sense the awesome glory of
God's presence surrounding you – so that you dare not open your eyes
for a moment or two.

PAUL GRAVELLE

Places of worship

As a deer longs for a stream of cool water, so I long for you, O God. I thirst for you, the living God. When can I go and worship in your presence?... My heart breaks when I remember the past, when I went with the crowds to the house of God and led them as they walked along, a happy crowd, singing and shouting praise to God.

While anywhere can be a place of worship, including your bedroom, a hilltop or a prison cell, we usually think of places of worship as cathedrals, churches and chapels. Some people feel that they can only worship in solitude, while others worship best in company with others. We should never forget that, like the exile who composed today's psalm, many of our Christian brothers and sisters across the world are in prison for their faith or are otherwise unable to gather in worship with others.

Most of us, however, are usually free to choose how and where we worship our Lord. Maybe we enjoy going into an older church building and sitting quietly in the atmosphere charged with the prayers of past generations of worshippers. I certainly love to do this when I can. If I am spending time alone with God and trying my best to give him the honour and reverence that is due to his name, the beauty of my surroundings is a blessed bonus. But my thoughts can't help but turn to those prison cells and to the writer of our psalm.

To worship alone is never enough. The reason we have 'places of worship' is so that we may come together to worship our God in community. In these days there are many countries where churches are being closed or even destroyed, so many of God's people are unable to gather together in this way. Let us thank God, therefore, for the freedom we still enjoy, make the most of that freedom and pray for all those who have none.

---

*Lord Jesus, some of your family are in prison or are forbidden
to gather together. They are in want of hope. Sustain them
with your everlasting faithfulness. Amen*

PAUL GRAVELLE

The disciples worship the Son

Between three and six o'clock in the morning Jesus came to the disciples, walking on the water. When they saw him walking on the water, they were terrified… Then Peter spoke up. 'Lord, if it is really you, order me to come out on the water to you.' 'Come!' answered Jesus. So Peter… started walking on the water to Jesus. But when he noticed the strong wind, he was afraid and started to sink down in the water. 'Save me, Lord!' he cried. At once Jesus reached out and grabbed hold of him… They both got into the boat, and the wind died down. Then the disciples in the boat worshipped Jesus. 'Truly you are the Son of God!' they exclaimed.

According to Matthew's account, this is one of the first occasions when the twelve had seen Jesus' supernatural powers in action. Their immediate response, once they recognised who was walking towards them on the water and calming the waves, was to worship him. As we read this story, I think we might want to amplify the dictionary definition of 'worship' with words like 'awe', 'respect' and 'honour'. I think I may be in danger sometimes of forgetting these aspects when I come to worship.

Try to put yourself in the place of those disciples in that boat. They had been terrified by seeing someone walking towards them on the waves, who then encouraged one of their number to do the same and then brought the wind and water to a flat calm. What else could they do but bow in total awe and respect, giving spellbound honour to this one whom they now recognised as the undoubted Son of God himself.

Even when I am in the place that I set aside as special to him, there are times when I can fail to be sufficiently aware of the one who is not only the miracle-working man of Galilee but also the creator of the entire universe. This is where the difference between praise and worship makes itself felt. Worship happens when, like the disciples, we become aware of who it is whose praises we are singing.

In what ways can you balance the awesome reverence of worship with the joyful exuberance of praise when you are in church? How could you blend these in your own personal devotion times?

PAUL GRAVELLE

Everything can be worship

So then, my friends, because of God's great mercy to us I appeal to you: Offer yourselves as a living sacrifice to God, dedicated to his service and pleasing to him. This is the true worship that you should offer. Do not conform yourselves to the standards of this world, but let God transform you inwardly by the complete change of your mind. Then you will be able to know the will of God – what is good and is pleasing to him and is perfect.

This is a tall order, although it's one that Brother Lawrence – the monk who scrubbed pots and pans in the kitchen to the glory of God – mastered to perfection. The apostle Paul is here suggesting that everything we do, whether at work, at home, out shopping or wherever, can be 'true worship'. He is, however, realistic about this – if what he suggests is to happen, we will need an inward transformation through a total mind-change.

Most of us, I trust, will find it relatively easy to be in an attitude of worship when we are in church or, as now, sitting quietly with *New Daylight* open. But what about when you are driving the car, sitting at your desk or trying to find a plumber to fix a leak in the bathroom? Surely it was easier for Brother Lawrence, who only had menial tasks to get through? How are we expected to follow Paul's directions in the context and complexities of 21st-century life? The answer, Paul says, is to 'let God transform you inwardly by the complete change of your mind'.

If this is the true worship we should offer, what might we need to let God do in us for that to happen? Have we yet discovered the kind of worship that God really wants? Paul's advice will surely lead us in the right direction.

'Teach me, my God and King, in all things thee to see,
and what I do in anything to do it as for thee.
A servant with this clause makes drudgery divine:
who sweeps a room, as for thy laws, makes that and th' action fine.'
('The Elixir', George Herbert, 1593–1633)

PAUL GRAVELLE

Holy, holy, holy, merciful and mighty

I will proclaim your greatness, my God and king; I will thank you forever and ever. Every day I will thank you; I will praise you forever and ever… What you have done will be praised from one generation to the next; they will proclaim your mighty acts. They will speak of your glory and majesty, and I will meditate on your wonderful deeds. People will speak of your mighty deeds, and I will proclaim your greatness. They will tell about all your goodness, and sing about your kindness.

In our church, we have a book containing about 50 hymns and songs that we use frequently. Looking through the index recently, I noticed that only about one in ten of them addressed words of praise directly to God. The psalmists seem to have had a similar reluctance, though Psalm 145 is one exception.

I am always ready to ask God to do things for me and to pray for my friends and family, for Christians undergoing persecution and for all manner of other needs that present themselves. I am not too bad at giving thanks too. There are always so many answers to prayer for which thanks are due. But when it comes to the simple matter of giving God the honour, reverence and homage that he deserves, I frequently find that I have forgotten to include that in my prayers altogether. Yet surely this is where I should begin – giving God the reverence and honour that is his due, with worship before his throne, before I present my requests?

I console myself, or rather make excuses, by saying that thanksgiving is really a form of worship. The psalmist in today's reading certainly speaks of what God has done, of his mighty acts and wonderful deeds, but he also pays homage to God's qualities of greatness, goodness and kindness.

Tomorrow, we will have a look at what Jesus himself had to say
on the subject. Meanwhile, let's use the words of one hymn writer
who has grasped what it means to give God the honour due to his name:
'Holy, Holy, Holy, Lord God Almighty!
Only thou art holy,
there is none beside thee'
(Reginald Heber, 1783–1826).

PAUL GRAVELLE

Jesus prioritises worship

One day Jesus was praying in a certain place. When he had finished, one of his disciples said to him, 'Lord, teach us to pray, just as John taught his disciples.' Jesus said to them, 'When you pray, say this: "Father: May your holy name be honoured; may your Kingdom come. Give us day by day the food we need. Forgive our sins, for we forgive everyone who does us wrong, And do not bring us to hard testing."'

Two simple statements of adoration and sheer worship before the petitioning begins – this is the pattern the disciples were taught to follow when one of them asked Jesus how they ought to pray. We are likely familiar with the longer version that appears in Matthew's gospel. While Matthew leaves the petitions as they are in Luke, he fills out the opening phrases of worship with the words 'may your will be done on earth as it is in heaven' (Matthew 6:10), for further emphasis. So this is the pattern: glory, reverence and honour to the one we are addressing, first and foremost, before anything else.

In the King James Version, we find a further addition, which concludes the prayer with even more words redolent with worshipful meaning: 'For thine is the kingdom, and the power, and the glory, forever. Amen' (v. 13). Biblical scholars think that final phrase was added later. At least it demonstrates that someone recognised Jesus' intention concerning the importance of giving full honour and reverence to the Father.

Jesus clearly wanted his followers to recognise the almighty power of the one whom we are invited to address as Father. The prayer teaches us the amazing paradox that the creator of our universe has a deep concern for the day-to-day details of our lives. For myself, I know I need to learn not to rush into the presence of the king of kings with my needs and requests without first giving him the honour, glory and reverence that are his due, forever and ever.

Father, may your holy name be honoured. May your kingdom come.
Meet the needs of your people everywhere, for yours is the kingdom,
the power and the glory, forever. Amen

PAUL GRAVELLE

Worship, pure and simple

A week later the disciples were together again indoors, and Thomas was with them. The doors were locked, but Jesus came and stood among them and said, 'Peace be with you.' Then he said to Thomas, 'Put your finger here, and look at my hands; then reach out your hand and put it in my side. Stop your doubting, and believe!' Thomas answered him, 'My Lord and my God!'

I like to imagine Thomas falling to his knees as he utters these words. They mark the moment of his conversion, of his step from unbelief into eternal life. But they are at the same time one of the simplest and purest expressions of worship that we will find anywhere.

Thomas has been the subject of many great sermons, but, whatever else we can learn from him, his recognition of Jesus as none other than God himself in human form and the sheer beauty of his submission to him as Lord are a perfect pattern for us as we seek to approach our God in worship.

When Jesus had earlier asked his disciples, 'Who do you say I am?', Peter's response was, 'You are the Messiah, the Son of the living God' (Matthew 16:15–16). Good try, Peter! But it took Thomas to come out with the full title that Jesus deserves: Lord and God – after all, nothing less will do.

There are moments for each of us when Thomas' simple yet profound act of worship is all that we need – maybe at the Communion rail or in our own quiet space – to bring us into the presence of Jesus or to become aware of the loving touch of the Father – 'My Lord and my God!' New Christians in those first days of the church would make a similar profession at their baptism. How happy Jesus must have been to hear those words then. He will be just as happy to hear them from you or me today.

Jesus, I know you are risen, alive at the right hand of the Father and that you will come again; you are my Lord and my God, forever and ever. Amen

PAUL GRAVELLE

Words of worship

How good it is to give thanks to you, O Lord, to sing in your honour, O Most High God, to proclaim your constant love every morning and your faithfulness every night, with the music of stringed instruments and with melody on the harp. Your mighty deeds, O Lord, make me glad; because of what you have done, I sing for joy. How great are your actions, Lord! How deep are your thoughts!

When we go to church, we are usually expected to sing. In fact we tend to use the term 'sung worship' for this part of the service, despite the fact that some songs are not strictly worship at all. I have recently started to pay more attention to the words of the hymns and songs that form part of the service and, as a result, have found it necessary to stop singing if and when the thoughts the songwriter is expressing are not ones that fit the way I am feeling towards God, others, the world or whatever. I am trying to teach myself not to sing the words mindlessly just because it is a Christian song.

On the other hand, of course, some hymns and Christian songs will make us think in new directions and open our minds to realise how great is our God and how unbelievably caring is his love for each of us, especially when things get hard.

Whether in hymns, songs, liturgy or extemporary prayers – and any or all of these can be worship in the broader sense – everyone needs to be involved. God can speak to each of us through any of these, and indeed any other medium. When we worship, it need never be one-way communication. What is more, when God speaks to groups or individuals, he can be relied upon to confirm his words, whether they are of help, encouragement or comfort, in more than one way. God is present when his people gather; expect to hear his voice speaking to you.

Lord God, I really want to hear what you are saying to me.
As I read, hear and sing words of worship, speak to me plainly
so that I can understand. Amen

PAUL GRAVELLE

Worship in the Spirit

[Jesus said,] 'But the time is coming and is already here, when by the power of God's Spirit people will worship the Father as he really is, offering him the true worship that he wants. God is Spirit, and only by the power of his Spirit can people worship him as he really is.'

We now come to an important aspect of personal worship that is a bit of a puzzle to some, just as what Jesus said to the Samaritan lady in today's verses seemed to mystify her. He couldn't say more at that time because this happened well before the coming of the Spirit at Pentecost, when believers first began to worship in this new, exciting way.

If I were asked to fill out what Jesus meant by 'worship in the power of the Spirit,' I would probably say something like this from my own experience: 'My English is limited. I don't have a vast vocabulary, particularly when it comes to worship. I do what I can with words like honour, might, goodness, faithfulness and so on. But my natural mind soon runs out, and I am just repeating myself. It is then that I need to allow the power of God's Spirit in me to take over the worshipping. So I simply offer the sound of my voice to God, so that, by the power of his Spirit, I can offer the Father "the true worship that he wants". I may not understand the meaning of the words I am saying to God in this way, but I can be entirely confident that what I say is in perfect accord with his will.'

Worship in the Spirit is a gift from God. God's people have been enjoying it since the day of Pentecost. Jesus says that only by the power of his Spirit can people offer the true worship that he wants, and I hope that we all want to offer that calibre of worship.

Why not offer some of the sounds of your voice to God's Spirit now (try the vowel sounds) and see what God might do?

PAUL GRAVELLE

Culture shock

David, wearing only a linen cloth around his waist, danced with all his might to honour the Lord. And so he and all the Israelites took the Covenant Box up to Jerusalem with shouts of joy and the sound of trumpets. As the Box was being brought into the city, Michal, Saul's daughter, looked out of the window and saw King David dancing and jumping around in the sacred dance, and she was disgusted with him.

It looks as if David might have been a bit over the top with his efforts to honour the Lord that day, and I can't help having some sympathy for Michal. It is always a bit of a culture shock when something out of the ordinary and which we are not used to happens in the context of worship.

I was brought up always to take my hat off when going into someone's house – particularly the house of God. So when some of our deeply worshipful young men began coming into church in beanies and baseball caps, sometimes not even uncovering at the Communion rail, I felt moved to say something about it – in other words, to 'do a Michal'. But that was the culture of their generation and, even if you think I did the right thing, I know that I did it in entirely the wrong way.

Things move fast these days. People will increasingly discover new ways of expressing their worship. If we were able to travel the world, we would find Christians in other countries who worship in ways that seem strange to us. And many of the things we do in church today would seem shocking to Christians of 100 years ago.

Many of us, including myself, need to learn that, just as people of many nations are worshipping in their own way the God whom we worship, so it is in different generations that differing cultures are to be found.

'After this I looked, and there was an enormous crowd… They were from every race, tribe, nation and language, and they stood in front of the throne… They called out in a loud voice: "Salvation comes from our God"' (Revelation 7:9–10).

PAUL GRAVELLE

Getting ready to worship

So then, you should each examine yourself first, and then eat the bread and drink from the cup. For if you do not recognise the meaning of the Lord's body when you eat the bread and drink from the cup, you bring judgement on yourself as you eat and drink. That is why many of you are sick and weak, and several have died. If we would examine ourselves first, we would not come under God's judgement.

When I was younger, getting ready for church meant wearing your best clothes (with no toy cars in the pockets), clean shoes and slicked-down hair. But the apostle Paul has a different concern here in writing to the church in Corinth. Communion was most likely the principal occasion for which they gathered to worship, and Paul discerned that some were coming with wrong attitudes.

Many churches today have a time for preparation and confession at the start of each service, which can be helpful in preparing for what is to follow. While we are promised that God is with us wherever we are, there is something extraordinarily special about assembling with others for worship and recognising his specific undertaking to be there whenever his people gather.

If we were invited to meet the sovereign, president, governor general or whoever the appropriate head of state might be, I'm sure we would seek to present ourselves in the best possible light. Paul's advice is even more appropriate when we go to meet with the king of kings.

Paul was not expecting God's people to die. He was expecting Jesus to return before that happened. It is in our future. When that happens, it will be a worship occasion like none other. All of the world's congregations, all those assemblies of worshippers from the past, from every nation and language, will be there to worship in unimaginable ways together. I cannot picture what that will be like, and we are not told very much about it in scripture, probably intentionally. The main thing is to be ready. Are you ready?

'Who has the right to go up the Lord's hill? Who may enter his holy Temple? Those who are pure in act and in thought, who do not worship idols or make false promises' (Psalm 24:3–4).

PAUL GRAVELLE

1 and 2 Timothy

 Receiving a personal letter by post is a rare thing these days. So much of our communication is done electronically that to have a non-Manila envelope plop through the letter box is a real treat. I almost always recognise the handwriting, so my anticipation is already high by the time I open the envelope.

Paul, the great apostle of the early Christian church, was a prolific letter writer. Such was his commitment to the believers in the churches he founded on his missionary journeys that he wrote extensively, covering varied topics from church life to personal greetings and insights.

One of the beauties of having the letters of 1 and 2 Timothy is their personal touch. Paul is writing to Timothy within the relationship they have developed. These two letters go way beyond matters of church business; they are written from the heart.

The two men had met in Timothy's home town of Lystra during Paul's first missionary journey. Timothy's conversion was genuine, and he matured rapidly in the faith, so that, when Paul returned some years later, the two of them paired up in ministry, travelling extensively through Asia Minor.

Paul's affection for Timothy shines through these two letters. Granted, there are tricky subjects that needed addressing. The Ephesian church was under attack from within, with influences from other religions undermining the true gospel. But the questions of what to believe and how to live out that faith have always lain at the heart of Christianity. We don't have to read very far before discovering that his message is every bit as relevant to us today.

In the first letter, Paul focuses on the heart. While the elders were busy misleading people with erroneous teaching, Paul emphasises the core messages of the gospel: love, integrity of character, concern for the lost and taking care of all generations within the fellowship.

By the time Paul wrote 2 Timothy, the apostle was nearing the end of his life, and there is noticeable urgency in his words. No matter how fierce the opposition, how difficult the circumstances, it was essential to keep fighting the good fight. The finish line was within Paul's sight. It was now up to Timothy to hold fast to the baton he'd been passed.

JANE WALTERS

Keeping our focus on the truth

As I urged you when I went into Macedonia, stay there in Ephesus so that you may command certain people not to teach false doctrines any longer or to devote themselves to myths and endless genealogies. Such things promote controversial speculations rather than advancing God's work – which is by faith. The goal of this command is love, which comes from a pure heart and a good conscience and a sincere faith.

In every church I've ever attended, there have been members who love nothing more than a good old argument. I don't mean a quarrel or a falling-out, but a love for vigorous discussion over some point or other. In my university days, our weekly Bible studies always drifted towards the topic of predestination, no matter where we'd started from. It was the pet topic of a particular core of students, and they couldn't switch off from it. It was an irritating rather than a harmful habit.

In today's passage, a group of Jewish Ephesian Christians, referred to namelessly as 'certain people' (since Timothy would know full well who Paul meant), were not pursuing the gospel truth but concentrating on a thorough study of the Old Testament, which led to an insistence on certain points of order from the law. Furthermore, they adopted allegorical interpretations of genealogy in the Pentateuch. These and other theological obsessions were not just distracting for the congregation under their care; they were also actively threatening to derail the fledgling faith of the Gentiles.

It's important, of course, that our faith be open to scrutiny and discussion. There is little merit in accepting facts blindly and without consideration. But there is a difference between digging more deeply into the scriptures to gain greater understanding and picking away at unnecessary detail for the sake of proving a point. We might tell ourselves that we are being diligent in keeping up with the latest thinking, but we need to be on constant guard that we don't somehow deaden the gospel for ourselves and others. After all, we should spend less time talking about theology and far more living out our faith.

Lord, help us to measure our ideas against the truth of your word.
Let our thinking be shaped and moulded by your truth,
and not the other way around. Amen

Dealing with the past

I thank Christ Jesus our Lord, who has given me strength, that he considered me trustworthy, appointing me to his service. Even though I was once a blasphemer and a persecutor and a violent man, I was shown mercy because I acted in ignorance and unbelief. The grace of our Lord was poured out on me abundantly, along with the faith and love that are in Christ Jesus.

During a weekend house party, our church had been listening to one of the young men tell the story of his dramatic conversion. Over coffee afterwards, I chatted with an older lady and bemoaned my lack of a sensational testimony. Her response was to tell me what the Lord had saved her from. It was quite a list: drunkenness, prostitution, theft and deceit. I must have been staring, because she began to laugh. 'Oh, my dear, I don't mean that I've done any of those things. No, they're the things the Lord has saved me from ever doing!'

Paul had one of the most powerful conversion experiences we can imagine. Stopped in his tracks on the road to Damascus, God took his murderous, hate-filled, prideful past and put within him a zeal for the gospel for which he would one day become a martyr. Nevertheless, there was no denying what Paul had once been and done. Everyone knew his past reputation. But far from letting it cause shame or embarrassment, Paul used it to proclaim the power of God's grace.

Perhaps there are things in our past that we regret and find it hard to forgive ourselves for and move on from. We can learn so much from Paul's approach. Aware of what others said behind his back, he knew the only solution was to offer all of it to God for him to deal with. Although our memories may make us feel ashamed, our mistakes can be the very things God uses to bring someone else closer to him. After all, if he could do it for Paul and me and you, he can do it for others, too.

Father, instead of hiding, we choose to offer you our regrets and mistakes. Please bring good out of them and let us experience your grace and mercy today. Amen

JANE WALTERS

Submission: the foundation for our worship

I urge, then, first of all, that petitions, prayers, intercession and thanksgiving be made for all people… that we may live peaceful and quiet lives in all godliness and holiness… Therefore I want the men everywhere to pray, lifting up holy hands without anger or disputing. I also want the women to dress modestly, with decency and propriety, adorning themselves, not with elaborate hairstyles or gold or pearls or expensive clothes, but with good deeds.

This chapter on 'instructions on worship' includes verses that female readers may find contentious. But it's important that we don't miss Paul's intention here: to encourage all believers to be prayerful and worshipping people who live as described above.

How should we do this? The key word is 'submission'. It's the reason that, for example, we pray for those in authority over us – not only because their leadership merits our respect, but also because we understand that they cannot do their job without our prayerful and practical support.

Paul's appeal to the men is interesting: not just that they should pray, but to do so with raised hands – a pose that demonstrates submission, even surrender. Choosing to pray in this way is a powerful statement that we're letting go of control and offering all the details of our lives to God. Note, too, that those raised hands are also empty hands; the weapons of anger and conflict have been laid down.

The instructions to the women are trickier. What does their clothing or hairstyle have to do with worship? The quick answer may be 'nothing', since the gospel invites us to come as we are, knowing that God accepts us in his love. But when we consider that Paul is writing about submitting ourselves in order to glorify Jesus, perhaps we should rethink how we dress: avoiding drawing attention to ourselves when our focus is on pointing others to God. Paul adds that women should clothe themselves in good deeds – their kindness and compassion bringing beauty to every situation. That is a fashion that will surely never date.

Jesus, let the way we live bring honour and glory to you. Help us to learn to submit to you and offer worship that is worthy of your name. Amen

JANE WALTERS

So you want to be a leader?

Here is a trustworthy saying: whoever aspires to be an overseer desires a noble task. Now the overseer is to be above reproach, faithful to his wife, temperate, self-controlled, respectable, hospitable, able to teach, not given to drunkenness, not violent but gentle, not quarrelsome, not a lover of money. He must manage his own family well… In the same way, deacons are to be worthy of respect, sincere, not indulging in much wine and not pursuing dishonest gain. They must keep hold of the deep truths of the faith with a clear conscience.

When my son was preparing to go to college, he began working at a fast-food restaurant to earn funds. He was skilled at the cooking, and soon he was asked if he would like to become a manager. At home, we laughed when he told us, but the truth was less funny. All the managers there were too young, lacking the experience and skill to handle their responsibilities and their staff. It was a recipe for disaster.

The apostle Paul knew that age is not a prerequisite for a church leader – after all, Timothy was still a young man. Rather, a church leader needs maturity of faith (v. 6). A well-rooted relationship with Jesus brings wisdom and resilience that go beyond confidence. Paul endured biting personal criticism and openly hostile persecution while dealing with the problems that cropped up in the churches he oversaw. A less mature leader might have thrown in the towel, but Paul chose to defend the gospel, even when he struggled to defend himself.

Paul offers sound advice when he says that potential leaders should first be capable of running their own homes well. Family life, conducted within the restrictions of a home's four walls, is the best training ground there could be. Nowhere else do we find the intensity of life at ground level, with its highs, lows and daily challenges. I've found that it's the best place to learn patience, forgiveness and the true meaning of love.

Father, we pray for our church leaders, that you would equip them with all they need to fulfil their responsibilities. Help us not to judge their shortcomings but to support them through prayer and by committing ourselves to their leadership. Amen

JANE WALTERS

Getting into training, and keeping going

Have nothing to do with godless myths and old wives' tales; rather, train yourself to be godly. For physical training is of some value, but godliness has value for all things, holding promise for both the present life and the life to come. This is a trustworthy saying that deserves full acceptance. That is why we labour and strive, because we have put our hope in the living God, who is the Saviour of all people, and especially of those who believe.

Training is such an important principle to understand. You see, learning a new skill is so much more than acquiring knowledge and understanding. One of my piano pupils, for example, may be completely aware of what they have to do, but being able to do it takes repetition, concentration and an overwriting of sometimes-obstructive natural instinct. In short, we are training our brains, minds and hands until the skill becomes second nature.

Paul begins this chapter by warning that there will be people who abandon their faith in favour of following flaky theology and superstition. It might feel easier to surround ourselves with mottos and sound bites, which we buy in gift shops and hang on our walls, than to train ourselves to pursue the truth; but the stakes are too high to ignore if we don't.

There is no doubt, of course, that training is hard work. It requires effort and stickability. If you're training for something, it simply isn't enough to go to the gym once a week (or, worse, to buy all the gear and not go at all). Nor is it enough to go to church once a week and not give God another thought between one Sunday and the next. At first, we may find new habits hard to cultivate, falling back into our familiar thought patterns, attitudes and behaviours. But, by focus and determination – and much prayer – we will get to the stage where we realise something has shifted and we no longer do things the way we used to.

Lord, we know that receiving salvation is just the start of our life's journey with you. Show us through your word where we need to make changes and get rid of bad habits. May our lives increasingly reflect Jesus within us. Amen

JANE WALTERS

It's not age but wisdom that counts

Don't let anyone look down on you because you are young, but set an example for the believers in speech, in conduct, in love, in faith and in purity. Until I come, devote yourself to the public reading of Scripture, to preaching and to teaching. Do not neglect your gift, which was given you through prophecy when the body of elders laid their hands on you. Be diligent in these matters; give yourself wholly to them, so that everyone may see your progress.

As I grow older, I find it increasingly difficult to guess someone's age. Fortunately, I tend to err on the cautious side, offering unwitting compliments to those I meet. But I've noticed something else: getting older is not the same as achieving maturity. Elihu recognised this, telling Job that it wasn't advancing years that brought wisdom, but the breath of God in a person (Job 32:7–8).

This explains how we can find extraordinary maturity in younger people. Timothy was such a man. A fair estimate of his age would be 30, perhaps not as young as we imagine, but certainly below the age of expected spiritual maturity at that time. His detractors would assume – perhaps naturally – that he was too young to do the job. But just as Elihu knew that it was God's touch on a life that did the transforming, so too Timothy had been equipped and enabled when he received not only the prophetic message that led him into church leadership but also the giftings he would need, imparted through the laying on of hands.

We glibly say, 'When God calls, he equips', and it is certainly true, but it merits further exploration. There would be no need for God to supply the equipment if we were already capable; there would be no requirement to be reliant on him or even to seek his help. As it is, God's call tends to draw us beyond our comfort zones and natural limits.

Lord, we thank you for the way you use us in achieving your purposes. Help us not to disqualify ourselves or others by having the wrong attitude. Instead, may we seek you for all we need in terms of wisdom and resources, knowing you delight to supply our needs. Amen

JANE WALTERS

Charity begins at home

Give proper recognition to those widows who are really in need. But if a widow has children or grandchildren, these should learn first of all to put their religion into practice by caring for their own family and so repaying their parents and grandparents, for this is pleasing to God... Anyone who does not provide for their relatives, and especially for their own household, has denied the faith and is worse than an unbeliever.

Under the Pharisees, the law of Moses had grown from the original ten commandments to over 600 rules and regulations. Jesus concentrated them into a couple of manageable principles, including this one: 'By this everyone will know that you are my disciples, if you love one another' (John 13:35).

While the Ephesians were busy with their theological debates, Paul reminds Timothy not to neglect the welfare of the church members. People in his congregation needed help, particularly the widows, whose social and financial standing would have been precarious at that time. But, just as he pointed out that a would-be deacon should first manage his home successfully (1 Timothy 3), Paul says here that the care of church members should begin within their own families. This putting into practice of their religion was evidence of their faith (v. 4).

Paul uses the phrase 'really in need' several times in 1 Timothy 5. Sadly, there will always be some who exploit the kindness of others, pushing themselves to the head of the queue. Timothy was to use discernment to ensure that help was always diverted to the right recipients, so that those in real hardship were properly supported.

Our society works somewhat differently to that of the early church. We tend to leave the care of the elderly to the professionals. We let the welfare state deal with poverty and hardship. But where the church has stepped in to plug the 'welfare gaps' with food banks and community support groups, we are once more showing the world what loving each other with the love of Jesus really means.

Father, help us not to wash our hands of our responsibility towards our own family members and those of our churches. Help us to demonstrate God's love in ways the world can see. Amen

JANE WALTERS

Keep your focus in the right place

If anyone teaches otherwise and does not agree to… godly teaching, they are conceited and understand nothing. They have an unhealthy interest in controversies and quarrels… that result in envy, strife, malicious talk, evil suspicions and constant friction between people of corrupt mind, who have been robbed of the truth and who think that godliness is a means to financial gain. But godliness with contentment is great gain… For the love of money is a root of all kinds of evil. Some people, eager for money, have wandered from the faith and pierced themselves with many griefs.

In an effort to make my life more efficient, I often turn to motivational books and seminars – trying to learn the secrets of success from those who know. The message that comes through loud and clear is not the one you might expect. Rather than developing our 'multitasking muscle', we achieve far more if we remain focused on one thing.

The Ephesian believers had their focus in the wrong place. By concentrating on trying to establish who was right, they achieved nothing but controversy, argument and division – hardly the hallmarks of a Christian church! Paul's advice to Timothy was to avoid these petty disputes and focus instead on the truth. This turns attention away from who is right towards what is right.

Moreover, the Ephesian elders had put an unhealthy emphasis on money: they were pursuing their idea of godliness in order to gain financially. This has been a constant distraction through the generations. Whether we call it the 'prosperity gospel' or simply hold the view that God's favour comes from pressing the right buttons, so to speak, the temptation to focus on what we can get out of faith is one we should guard carefully against.

Jesus' words sum it up perfectly for me: 'Seek first his kingdom and his righteousness, and all these things will be given to you as well' (Matthew 6:33).

Jesus, help us today to fix our eyes on you. Don't let us be sidetracked from the truth or pulled into petty argument. We worship you for who you are, not for what you can do for us. Amen

JANE WALTERS

Make sure you reach the goal

But you, man of God, flee from all this, and pursue righteousness, godliness, faith, love, endurance and gentleness. Fight the good fight of the faith. Take hold of the eternal life to which you were called when you made your good confession in the presence of many witnesses… Timothy, guard what has been entrusted to your care. Turn away from godless chatter and the opposing ideas of what is falsely called knowledge.

I'm not a particular fan of rugby, but nevertheless I have watched the moment when a player has taken possession of the ball and runs the length of the pitch to score a try. Opposing players appear on all sides, grabbing at him, but nothing makes him so much as slow down. Eyes on the line, he ignores his own physical pain and those attempts to get the ball and keeps on running.

Paul's tone is urgent in today's passage: 'Flee from all this… Fight the good fight… Take hold… Guard.' These are not mere suggestions with a take-it-or-leave-it option for responding. Difficult times call for definitive measures, and this is such a moment for Timothy.

In previous days we read how the Ephesians had swallowed the half-truths and flaky beliefs the elders fed them. Their thinking would have shifted gradually, perhaps almost imperceptibly, and they will not have realised the harm they were doing to themselves. But now Paul is delivering a wake-up call. It's time for action, not just to flee from the lies but also to pursue those qualities listed above.

Timothy was to grab hold of the eternal life he was called to and run with it. While some put their trust in wealth, believing it will see them through life's hard times, Timothy was to demonstrate what a foundation based on hope in God looked like. He may not have had money in the bank to secure his future, but he had a legacy of faith stretching back his entire life and extending forwards into the rest of his days.

Jesus, help us to let go of all those things which lead us away from you, and may we 'take hold of the life that is truly life' (v. 19). Amen

JANE WALTERS

Keeping our fires burning

For this reason I remind you to fan into flame the gift of God, which is in you through the laying on of my hands. For the Spirit God gave us does not make us timid, but gives us power, love and self-discipline. So do not be ashamed of the testimony about our Lord or of me his prisoner. Rather, join with me in suffering for the gospel, by the power of God.

Paul's analogy of fire is a helpful and vivid one. Lighting a coal fire, for example, begins with stacking wooden kindling or twists of paper. They light easily but, without adding coal at the right moment, they soon burn through and the fire goes out. Timothy's foundation of faith, rooted in his upbringing by a Christian mother and grandmother, had got him started on a lifetime of serving God, but he needed fuel to keep burning. This had come when Paul had laid hands on Timothy at some point, imparting spiritual gifts as well as a commission. It provided the fire within his heart that enabled him to minister in difficult situations despite his relative youth.

But Paul knew that fire can be put out. Sometimes, in fact, the very act of adding too much wood or coal too soon can choke the flames instead of stoking them. And, of course, it's possible to pour cold water on flames, reducing them to a sizzle in moments. Fear can act as water on our inner fire. We might feel a burning within us as we sense God's call or hear his word. We can get 'all fired up' with missionary zeal, only to find that our passions fizzle away at the first sign of opposition or when anxiety creeps in and erodes our confidence. This is why Paul reminds not only Timothy but also us today that we have been given a spirit of power, love and self-discipline – good fuel to be added to a well-built fire.

Lord, we want to be people that burn steadily for you, providing light and warmth to the world around us, and remaining enthusiastic. Fill us with your Holy Spirit, so that we don't burn up or burn out. Amen

JANE WALTERS

Free indeed

Reflect on what I am saying, for the Lord will give you insight into all this. Remember Jesus Christ, raised from the dead, descended from David. This is my gospel, for which I am suffering even to the point of being chained like a criminal. But God's word is not chained. Therefore I endure everything for the sake of the elect, that they too may obtain the salvation that is in Christ Jesus, with eternal glory.

Paul's focus in these letters has been almost exclusively on Timothy. Concentrating on helping this young pastor deal with his church, Paul has only made brief references to himself. Now we read this description of him 'chained like a criminal' and its powerful, visual impression stops us in our tracks. Here is a man, not just under house arrest as he was previously, but under guard and in manacles.

One of the deep mysteries of God is that he continues to work despite seemingly impossible situations. Into my mind comes immediately the story of Corrie ten Boom, held in one of the terrible concentration camps during World War II. Along with her sister, she saw incredible evidence of God working among them. They might not have had their freedom, but God is not restricted by man-made barriers.

It's hard to square Paul's optimism and enthusiasm with his surroundings in the letters he wrote while incarcerated. But this was the secret: God's word is not chained. I repeat, God's word is not chained. We can ban the sale of Bibles, making it a criminal offence to take them across international borders; we can forbid the public meeting of believers and prosecute those who share their faith; but the word of God cannot be stopped.

It was Paul's deep-rooted understanding of this that led him to continue: 'Therefore I endure everything.' No hardship or loss of privilege is too great when the reward is to see many saved.

Lord, we pray for all believers in prison: those who are imprisoned for their faith and those who have come to know you while serving their sentence. We ask that you give them a sense of freedom despite their confinement and that they may know the joy of your presence. Amen

JANE WALTERS

'O use me, Lord, use even me'

Do your best to present yourself to God as one approved, a worker who does not need to be ashamed and who correctly handles the word of truth... In a large house there are articles not only of gold and silver, but also of wood and clay; some are for special purposes and some for common use. Those who cleanse themselves from the latter will be instruments for special purposes, made holy, useful to the Master and prepared to do any good work.

In the fervency of my early Christian years, the hymns of Frances Ridley Havergal had a huge impact on my growing faith, with lines like 'Take my life, and let it be consecrated, Lord, to thee', 'I am trusting thee to guide me; thou alone shalt lead' and 'O use me, Lord, use even me'.

It was this last one that would choke me as I prayed it, desperate for the Lord to 'pick me for his team'. Years of preparation followed that yearning of my heart, frustrating for this young woman eager to make an impact on her world.

The fact is that, no matter how keen we are to serve God, we can't do so until he has made us ready. Moses was an old man by the time he led the people out of Egypt. Abraham was a father at an age that some of us merely aspire to. Despite the world favouring the young, sometimes it simply takes a long time to change those vessels of wood and clay into something more precious, more valuable and more useful.

When we're in a season of non-activity, which God might more correctly call 'preparation', we can quickly grow impatient. In our eagerness to make something happen, some of us leap into roles we were never destined for, perhaps thereby blocking someone else from their true calling. We can't rush the process. Let God be God.

Lord, we trust you to guide and lead us into all you have for us. Forgive us for trying to create our own opportunities instead of waiting for your invitation. We know that you have good plans for us, ones we may not be quite ready for. We submit ourselves to your will. Amen

JANE WALTERS

God's timeless message to the world

But as for you, continue in what you have learned and have become convinced of, because you know those from whom you learned it, and how from infancy you have known the Holy Scriptures, which are able to make you wise for salvation through faith in Christ Jesus. All Scripture is God-breathed and is useful for teaching, rebuking, correcting and training in righteousness, so that the servant of God may be thoroughly equipped for every good work.

I recently read a book challenging the self-centredness of our society, with its focus on self-reliance, self-belief and self-confidence. We can press an icon on our phones that switches the camera to face ourselves; unwittingly, we have extended that practice into other areas of our lives.

The church is not immune from this shift in perspective. Worship songs have become increasingly 'me-centred' instead of 'God-centred'. We sing of how we feel about loving God rather than offering our praise and adoration directly to him. When we read our Bibles, it's in the hope of receiving a word that speaks to our personal situation. Without wishing to sound too controversial, is this so very different from those who read their horoscope?

Today's verses remind us that scripture is so much more than our personal guidebook. Its wisdom supersedes that of any generation or culture. In fact, it often runs against the tide, reminding us of God's ageless, never-changing standards and principles. How many of us read the Bible hoping that we will be corrected or rebuked? And yet, without constantly comparing ourselves to the benchmark that is God himself, our faith will be based on opinion, supposition and even superstition.

Paul's message to the Ephesian church through his letters to Timothy has been focused on holding true to the gospel. We mustn't think ourselves immune from the sideways or even downwards slip into the world's standards. Let us continue to read God's word expecting him to speak to us, whether that be in encouragement or challenge.

'Search me, God, and know my heart; test me and know my anxious thoughts. See if there is any offensive way in me, and lead me in the way everlasting' (Psalm 139:23–24).

JANE WALTERS

51

Keep on keeping on

In the presence of God and of Christ Jesus, who will judge the living and the dead, and in view of his appearing and his kingdom, I give you this charge: preach the word; be prepared in season and out of season; correct, rebuke and encourage – with great patience and careful instruction. For the time will come when people will not put up with sound doctrine... But you, keep your head in all situations, endure hardship, do the work of an evangelist, discharge all the duties of your ministry.

The final chapter of Paul's letters to Timothy offers a summary of his main points: do what you know you're supposed to be doing; do it well; and keep on doing it.

Under the heading 'do it well', we have to take note of Paul's phrase 'with great patience and careful instruction'. As all teachers know, unless we teach with patience – aware of our pupils' anxiety or lack of confidence – we are unlikely to be successful. This applies very much within church, too. When preachers and teachers are only focused on their own delivery and, dare we say, performance, they miss the needs of their congregation. This doesn't mean ignoring difficult topics for fear of causing offence, but requires us to tackle everything sensitively, carefully.

Paul's instruction to 'keep your head in all situations' might induce thoughts of Lance Corporal Jack Jones in *Dad's Army* running around crying, 'Don't panic! Don't panic!' But, all joking aside, sometimes the only way forward is to set our course, put one foot in front of the other and keep moving. We need faith, most certainly, but determination plays its part, too. The personal greetings Paul goes on to bring at the end of the chapter are a reminder that opposition can come even from our friends. Friendly fire is perhaps the most damaging kind, but Paul could attest, 'The Lord stood at my side and gave me strength' (v. 17). He was able to keep on keeping on.

Father, help us to be aware of the needs of those around us as we live out our calling. Help us to remember who it is we're serving, and give us grace, strength and determination to continue. For Jesus' sake. Amen

JANE WALTERS

2 Kings

The book of 2 Kings tells the story of the kings of Israel and Judah up to the time when both kingdoms, first Israel and then Judah, were conquered by foreign powers and their peoples taken into exile. It is not an easy book to read for several reasons. It starts abruptly: 1 and 2 Kings are really all one story, covering 400 years of history from c. 960BC to c. 586BC. Kings are frequently introduced with the words, 'He did what was evil in the sight of the Lord.' These are God's people, whom he chose and whom he loves; how can things have got so bad? And the thread can be hard to follow, as the narrator describes first the reign of a king of Israel, then moves to the king of Judah who started to rule during his reign, and so on, backwards and forwards.

We may be living thousands of years later, but we can relate to a world of inequality, violence and suffering, where some of those in power oppress their people, where God's commandments are flouted and where God's followers face mockery and worse. Where is God? My hope is that we will be encouraged as we read of the men and women who kept the rumour of God alive amid so much disobedience.

The twists and turns of the story reflect how much (or not) kings are faithful to God and reject the gods of their neighbours. While we may struggle with the theme of judgement, we are encouraged to see it as something that a series of kings have brought on themselves, with just a few remaining faithful to God.

I have included a few of the darker moments, but primarily we will focus on God's prophet Elisha, who performs many miracles, pointing to God and protecting the nation; Naaman the Syrian, who found faith; and the later kings Hezekiah and Josiah, whose reigns of faithfulness contrast with the gloom of the rest. God is infinitely patient, but after the people's many broken promises and utter rejection of God's ways, grace and mercy give way to judgement at the end of the book. Even in exile, though, there is a glimmer of hope. God can bring good out of even the bleakest situation.

ROSIE WARD

Elisha succeeds Elijah

Elijah said to Elisha, 'Tell me what I may do for you, before I am taken from you.' Elisha said, 'Please let me inherit a double share of your spirit.' He responded… 'If you see me as I am being taken from you, it will be granted you…' As they continued walking and talking, a chariot of fire and horses of fire separated the two of them, and Elijah ascended in a whirlwind into heaven. Elisha… took the mantle of Elijah that had fallen from him, and struck the water, saying, 'Where is the Lord, the God of Elijah?' When he had struck the water, the water was parted to the one side and to the other, and Elisha went over.

Amid the troubled times after King Solomon, the rumour of God was kept alive primarily by the prophet Elijah. The book of 2 Kings begins with the king of Israel turning away from God to Baal-zebub, and Elijah showing God's power. So when we read, 'The Lord was about to take Elijah up to heaven' (v. 1), the tension is building. What will happen when Elijah is no longer around to speak for God?

The answer is his successor, Elisha. The mantle is passed from Elijah to Elisha. Whatever Elijah could do, Elisha could do too. Elisha parts the water and goes through – recalling the parting of the Jordan when Israel entered Canaan (Joshua 3—4). It's a reminder that despite the sorry state of Israel (and Judah), God is still as mighty in 850BC as when his people entered the promised land. His servants can still demonstrate God's mighty power. And the change of prophet is also a reminder that the miracles are all about God and not whichever leader or prophet it is.

In our churches, when we face a change of leader, it's all too easy to approach their departure with trepidation. Will the new man or woman be like their predecessor, the one we've become so used to and attached to? Of course they won't. The challenge for us may be to trust not in the charisma of God's servants, but in God himself. Change happens, but God is changeless.

Where does my trust lie? In human leaders or in the God they serve?

ROSIE WARD

Does God care?

Now the wife of a member of the company of prophets cried to Elisha, 'Your servant my husband is dead; and you know that your servant feared the Lord, but a creditor has come to take my two children as slaves.' Elisha said to her, 'What shall I do for you? Tell me, what do you have in the house?' She answered, 'Your servant has nothing in the house, except a jar of oil.' He said, 'Go outside, borrow vessels from all your neighbours… Then go in, and shut the door behind you and your children, and start pouring into all these vessels; when each is full, set it aside.' So she left him and shut the door behind her and her children; they kept bringing vessels to her, and she kept pouring… Then the oil stopped flowing. She came and told the man of God, and he said, 'Go, sell the oil and pay your debts, and you and your children can live on the rest.'

For so many people, life seems unfair. This woman is doubly desperate: she has lost her husband through death, and she is threatened with losing her sons through slavery (slavery for debt was part of the Hebrew legal system). But she and her husband had trusted God, and so in her anguish the widow turns to him, in the form of his prophet Elisha.

As Jesus does with the bread and fish in Mark 6:38, Elisha asks what the woman has already, and he works with that. It's a sign of her destitution that she has nothing but a jar of oil. When she borrows more vessels, the oil keeps coming. There's enough to sell to both pay the debt and live on for the future. God is a generous God, who gives more and more, blessing us to overflowing.

As we cry out to God on behalf of all those who are in need today, perhaps this can answer our question: does God care for desperate people? Yes, he does. He may do it today by using our prayers or using us to give food and water, seeds or chickens or goats which multiply, but the miracle is the same.

How can I demonstrate God's care for those in desperate need?

ROSIE WARD

When tragedy strikes

When the child was older, he went out one day to his father among the reapers. He complained to his father, 'Oh, my head, my head!' The father said to his servant, 'Carry him to his mother'… The child sat on her lap until noon, and he died… When Elisha came into the house, he saw the child lying dead on his bed. So he went in and closed the door on the two of them, and prayed to the Lord. Then he got up on the bed and lay upon the child, putting his mouth upon his mouth… and while he lay bent over him, the flesh of the child became warm. He got down, walked once to and fro in the room, then got up again and bent over him; the child sneezed seven times, and the child opened his eyes.

Whenever Elisha travelled through Shunem (south-west of the Sea of Galilee), he stayed at the home of a woman who offered him hospitality. She even built a room on the roof for him to use. How could Elisha reward her? She was childless, and her husband was old. But that was no problem to God. Elisha told her that next year she would have a son, and so it was. The Bible recounts several stories of barren women who give birth: Sarah, Hannah and Elizabeth, to name just three. Only in this case, the boy was not part of the wider story. The miracle took place simply to bring one family joy.

But then tragedy strikes. And perhaps the very gift of a son seemed like a sick joke, when his life was so cruelly taken away. His mother must have been distraught – but her faith holds as she travels some distance to find the man of God.

When trouble comes, where can we go? It must have taken all of her faith to keep trusting, but the woman's trust is rewarded. Elisha arrives, and by God's power the boy is raised to life. Sneezes never sounded so healthy! This story is also a foretaste of resurrection to come. In God's story, death will not have the last word.

'I believe in the sun, even when it is not shining.
I believe in God, even when he is silent' (Anonymous).

ROSIE WARD

Enough and to spare

A man came from Baal-shalishah, bringing food from the first fruits to the man of God: twenty loaves of barley and fresh ears of grain in his sack. Elisha said, 'Give it to the people and let them eat.' But his servant said, 'How can I set this before a hundred people?' So he repeated, 'Give it to the people and let them eat, for thus says the Lord, "They shall eat and have some left."' He set it before them, they ate, and had some left, according to the word of the Lord.

Several of the stories about Elijah and Elisha have to do with food. In an agrarian community, starvation was never far away, as for many in our world today. And with changing weather patterns due to climate change, increasing numbers will face starvation.

Here in the time of Elisha, there is a famine in the land, so food is top of the agenda. After a miracle in which he renders harmless a pot of poisonous stew (vv. 38–41), Elisha is faced with the problem of feeding a hundred people with a small amount of food, a situation familiar to us from stories of Jesus feeding four or five thousand. Notice the mention of first fruits brought to Elisha. The law in Deuteronomy specifies that they should go to the priests, so what is happening? It seems that the man is recognising Elisha as the one representative of God in the land amid so much that is ungodly, taking the place of the priests who had compromised themselves by association with Baal worship.

Elisha instructs the people to eat, a hundred symbolising a large number or totality, and tells them that God promises enough to eat and some left over – as there is in Jesus' miracles of feeding.

As Christians we are not immune from need or even starvation, but we have a God who is not stymied by our inadequacies. Humble barley loaves aren't much to work with, but God doesn't need much. He seems to like doing big things through little things. Our talents and resources may seem small, but in the face of what God can do with them, they are enough.

'Take my life, and let it be consecrated, Lord, to thee'
(Frances Ridley Havergal, 1836–79).

ROSIE WARD

The little girl, the general and God

Naaman, commander of the army of the king of Aram, was a great man and in high favour with his master, because by him the Lord had given victory to Aram. The man, though a mighty warrior, suffered from leprosy. Now the Arameans on one of their raids had taken a young girl captive from the land of Israel, and she served Naaman's wife. She said to her mistress, 'If only my lord were with the prophet who is in Samaria! He would cure him of his leprosy.'

No prophet performed as many miracles as Elisha. At one point in the narrative, the king of Israel says to Gehazi, Elisha's servant, 'Tell me all the great things that Elisha has done' (2 Kings 8:4). There are plenty. One which stands out is the story of Naaman.

The young girl is one of those unnamed but special people in the Bible. She has been captured in a raid, taken away from everyone she knows and from her homeland and set to work as a slave for the wife of a foreigner. We can only imagine how hard that must have been for a child. But she has not forgotten her homeland or the 'prophet who is in Samaria' who was manifesting God's power in Israel – the same Lord who 'had given victory to Aram', the narrator reminds us. The girl is quick to suggest that Elisha might be the only person powerful enough to help. As a result of her words Naaman sets off for Israel, to seek out this prophet.

Naaman's miraculous healing would lead to his becoming a worshipper of the Lord. It all began with the testimony of a young girl who had faith in God and confidence in the power of God's prophet. In the following verses, when the king of Israel receives a letter from the king of Aram, saying that Naaman is coming to be cured of leprosy, the king is alarmed. The believing maid is contrasted with the frightened king. Young and female, this girl was doubly unimportant in the eyes of many. But how often God entrusts the young, the forgotten and the humble with important tasks!

'Unless you change and become like children,
you will never enter the kingdom of heaven' (Matthew 18:3).

ROSIE WARD

Grace goes international

But his servants approached and said to [Naaman], 'Father, if the prophet had commanded you to do something difficult, would you not have done it? How much more, when all he said to you was, "Wash, and be clean"?' So he went down and immersed himself seven times in the Jordan, according to the word of the man of God; his flesh was restored like the flesh of a young boy, and he was clean.

Naaman is doubly an outsider. He is Aramean and has a skin disease (though not necessarily leprosy; we are told that when Elisha's servant is made leprous, his skin is 'white as snow' (v. 27), and the lesions of true leprosy are not white). Finally getting to Elisha's house, Naaman, full of his own importance, is not impressed by what happens next. Elisha sends a messenger to him, instructing him to wash in the River Jordan. In storytelling terms it's a classic narrative test: do something that appears silly. Naaman expected at least to see the prophet himself, and complained that the rivers of his own country were much better than 'all the waters of Israel' (v. 12).

But here again it is the supposedly unimportant people, this time Naaman's servants, who help the general to see sense. And he is made clean – not because the Jordan is any better than the rivers of Syria, but by simple obedience. It's a story quoted in the New Testament (Luke 4:27) as an example of the healing of a Gentile. God is not just the God of Israel.

And that insight into God is a part of Naaman's own response. After the miracle, Naaman's thoughts move swiftly. He recognises that God is bigger than a local deity: 'Now I know that there is no God in all the earth except in Israel' (v. 15). Israel's god is the one true God. The Lord is God not just of Israelites, but of foreigners, and acknowledged as the only real God. It is deeply ironic that in the midst of so much idolatry on the part of Israel, such an outstanding statement should come from the lips of a foreigner.

Lord, we long that all may know you, the one true God.

ROSIE WARD

When I bow down

Then Naaman said… 'Please let two mule-loads of earth be given to your servant; for your servant will no longer offer burnt-offering or sacrifice to any god except the Lord. But may the Lord pardon your servant on one count: when my master goes into the house of Rimmon to worship there, leaning on my arm, and I bow down in the house of Rimmon, when I do bow down in the house of Rimmon, may the Lord pardon your servant on this one count.' He said to him, 'Go in peace.'

It's a swift change of allegiance. First Naaman despised the Jordan and everything about Israel; now he asks Elisha if he can take some of the earth from Israel home with him! He has also changed from arrogance to humility. But what is the significance of the earth which he wants to take on his mules?

The soil sample will tie Naaman to the land of Israel and be a tangible reminder of his faith, a kind of icon of the divine presence. Even though he knows that God is God of all the earth, he still wants something physical to help him. The exiles were to face the same dilemma: 'How could we sing the Lord's song in a foreign land?' (Psalm 137:4). Far from Jerusalem, they felt unable to worship. We know that God is not found in physical objects, but we may still cherish things which remind us of our spiritual journey.

Naaman is going back to Aram, where he says that he will worship only the true God. But he is wise enough to see that this may involve compromise. He will have to go into the temple of Rimmon (another name for Hadad, the Syrian god of storm and thunder). Later, Corinthian Christians agonised over meat offered to idols, and today Christians may be obliged to take part in rituals in temples or other religious buildings. It's a very real question still: which compromises are legitimate, and which are betrayals of faith? Naaman needs pardon for a compromise he knows is imperfect. Faced with divided loyalties, there are no easy answers.

Pray for those making everyday decisions about how they express their faith in hostile environments.

ROSIE WARD

Famine, food and faith

Some time later King Ben-hadad of Aram mustered his entire army; he marched against Samaria and laid siege to it… Famine in Samaria became so great that a donkey's head was sold for eighty shekels of silver, and one-fourth of a kab of dove's dung for five shekels of silver… But Elisha said, 'Hear the word of the Lord: thus says the Lord, Tomorrow about this time a measure of choice meal shall be sold for a shekel, and two measures of barley for a shekel…' Then the captain on whose hand the king leaned said to the man of God, 'Even if the Lord were to make windows in the sky, could such a thing happen?' But he said, 'You shall see it with your own eyes, but you shall not eat from it.'

The Arameans, a people from the north (in what we now call Syria) kept attacking Israel, and Elisha helped Israel to thwart them. Aram then attacks again, and the famine becomes severe. The cost of food reflects its shortage, and some people resort to cannibalism (6:28–29). They are desperate. Only a miracle can save them.

The king of Israel, Jehoram, blames God and sends someone to kill Elisha. He no longer expects God to rescue him and his people, but Elisha promises that by the next day things will have changed. The captain expresses his disbelief, but God acts: the Aramean army flees. And as the people of Israel rush to plunder the enemy's camp, the captain is trampled to death in the gateway.

It was an astounding promise of deliverance. Hard to believe? But the fate of the captain is a reminder that to doubt the prophetic word is to mock God. The New Testament expects faith – but the Old Testament does too. God is the same God, the one who sent his Son to bring ultimate deliverance from sin through his death and then raised him to life. What God says, he will do. God has made many promises in his word. Do we trust them?

'Our help is in the name of the Lord, who made heaven and earth'
(Psalm 124:8).

ROSIE WARD

Resurrection

Now when Elisha had fallen sick with the illness of which he was to die, King Joash of Israel went down to him, and wept before him, crying, 'My father, my father! The chariots of Israel and its horsemen!'… So Elisha died, and they buried him. Now bands of Moabites used to invade the land in the spring of the year. As a man was being buried, a marauding band was seen and the man was thrown into the grave of Elisha; as soon as the man touched the bones of Elisha, he came to life and stood on his feet.

The prophet Elisha fell ill at a time when Israel's chariots and horsemen had been decimated by the Arameans. Hence the visit from King Joash, hoping for the usual divine intervention. The king's partial obedience of Elisha's instructions led to partial success. But with the death of Elisha, Israel was losing the man who had tried his hardest to keep the nation in God's ways. What would happen now? Was there any hope for Israel? Time would tell. But here, two verses tell a remarkable story about a corpse being hastily thrown into Elisha's tomb (probably in a cave); it resulted in resurrection.

Down the centuries there have been many stories about relics and objects with healing properties, which are often dismissed as superstition. Acts 19:11–12 describes how handkerchiefs and work aprons were carried from Paul's body to the sick and appeared to heal them. Even in Elisha's death, God's power is still available for Israel. Elisha may be dead, but the God of Elisha is as powerful as ever, which must have brought hope to those with the faith to believe it.

Elijah did not die, but was taken up to heaven. Elisha died, and then through his body God worked a miracle. These are small pictures of the day when one man who walked out of a tomb would destroy death itself and bring resurrection for the whole world. In the meantime, as we pray for healing, we can trust in the same God of miracles.

Healing God, by your resurrection power bring wholeness of body, mind and spirit to those for whom we pray. Amen

ROSIE WARD

'You, O Lord, are God alone'

Hezekiah prayed before the Lord, and said: 'O Lord the God of Israel, who are enthroned above the cherubim, you are God, you alone, of all the kingdoms of the earth; you have made heaven and earth. Incline your ear, O Lord, and hear; open your eyes, O Lord, and see; hear the words of Sennacherib, which he has sent to mock the living God. Truly, O Lord, the kings of Assyria have laid waste the nations and their lands, and have hurled their gods into the fire, though they were no gods but the work of human hands – wood and stone – and so they were destroyed. So now, O Lord our God, save us, I pray you, from his hand, so that all the kingdoms of the earth may know that you, O Lord, are God alone.'

The Assyrians were the most powerful nation around by this time, and after a three-year attack on Samaria, the capital fell and the Israelites were exiled. The narrative turns to the small southern kingdom of Judah, which carried David's line. King Hezekiah put right some (but not all) of what his predecessors had done wrong. And whereas some of them failed to turn to God, even in a crisis, Hezekiah's response to the king of Assyria's threats was to pray to the Lord.

I have been struck by the Methodist tradition of starting worship with a prayer of adoration or praise. It's the prelude to prayers of petition and intercession – prayers for ourselves and for others. As we focus on God's majesty, glory and power, we are reminded of all that he is and all that he has done. Then we can trust him to help us, even when the situation looks bleak and hopeless.

God is near, vast and mighty – and Hezekiah's only hope. In the narrative, Hezekiah's prayer is answered by words of God delivered by the prophet Isaiah, a promise of hope for Jerusalem and the nation: 'I will defend this city to save it, for my own sake and for the sake of my servant David' (v. 34). That night the Assyrian troops are struck down in the camp, and King Sennacherib goes home to Nineveh.

How might taking a long look at God help us as we come to pray?

ROSIE WARD

Who speaks for God?

'Go and enquire of the Lord for me and for the people and for all Judah about what is written in this book that has been found. Great is the Lord's anger that burns against us because those who have gone before us have not obeyed the words of this book; they have not acted in accordance with all that is written there concerning us.' Hilkiah the priest, Ahikam, Akbor, Shaphan and Asaiah went to speak to the prophet Huldah, who was the wife of Shallum son of Tikvah, the son of Harhas, keeper of the wardrobe. She lived in Jerusalem, in the New Quarter.

King Josiah was desperate. He was a God-fearing man, and now, trying to rid God's people of idols, he realised that his people were in a worse situation than he had thought: the book of the law of God clearly told God's people how to live, and how far from it they had strayed!

Nothing in the text indicates that the high officials had any qualms consulting Huldah. She was clearly a recognised prophet whom they could consult when something as essential as the book of the law of God had been rediscovered. Huldah ranks with Deborah among the rare women in the Old Testament to have a formal leadership role.

We should be careful not to discount the more unlikely people who speak for God or bring spiritual wisdom. In some churches, women are still overlooked in favour of men. Some years ago, when I talked to a group of women church planters, one of them showed me a cartoon captioned: 'A church plant? That's an excellent suggestion, Miss MacAdams. Perhaps one of the men would like to make it.'

Gender, race, age and background can all be reasons why we may overlook people who speak for God. At the same time, we should not discount ourselves, thinking that God could not speak through us. We need to be ready to speak up at the right time, when we know that our wisdom is recognised and an important moment has come.

May we be attuned to those who bring a word from God –
and open to that person being us.

ROSIE WARD

Josiah reads the book

The king went up to the house of the Lord, and with him went all the people of Judah… He read in their hearing all the words of the book of the covenant that had been found in the house of the Lord. The king stood by the pillar and made a covenant before the Lord, to follow the Lord, keeping his commandments, his decrees and his statutes, with all his heart and all his soul, to perform the words of this covenant that were written in this book. All the people joined in the covenant.

The reign of Josiah followed those of Manasseh and Amon, kings who 'did what was evil in the sight of the Lord' (21:2, 20). The nation had rejected God so thoroughly that judgement had been announced, and it was just a question of time. But at the eleventh hour, Judah found itself with a righteous king, the best of all kings, one of only three kings to share a favourable comparison with David, the touchstone for all the kings of Israel and Judah. The book he discovered was the book of Deuteronomy, or a substantial part of it, God's word to his people.

As a reader of these notes, you already know the importance of God's word. Hearing it read is valuable, as is reading it on our own. But like Josiah, we can find ourselves reading things in God's word that are not what we want to hear. When I first felt God calling me to authorised ministry my initial response was a feeling of inadequacy. I lacked confidence and felt that that was a good excuse for ignoring God's nudge. But it seemed that every time I opened a Bible or a Christian book I read about Moses, whose lack of eloquence was no problem to God. I had to admit defeat and be obedient to the call.

Whether we need courage in our fear, light in our darkness or reassurance in our sense of unworthiness, we can find it all in scripture. But, hearing God's word, we must also act on it.

'Speak, Lord, in the stillness, while I wait on thee; hushed my heart to listen in expectancy' (Emily Crawford, 1864–1927).

ROSIE WARD

The path of obedience

The king commanded all the people, 'Keep the passover to the Lord your God as prescribed in this book of the covenant.' No such passover had been kept since the days of the judges who judged Israel, even during all the days of the kings of Israel and of the kings of Judah; but in the eighteenth year of King Josiah this passover was kept to the Lord in Jerusalem. Moreover, Josiah did away with the mediums, wizards, teraphim, idols and all the abominations that were seen in the land of Judah and in Jerusalem, so that he established the words of the law that were written in the book that the priest Hilkiah had found in the house of the Lord.

Are you one of those people who only slows down when you know the speed camera is working or only returns the wallet you found to its owner if there's a reward? Or do you do the right thing anyway?

Josiah's reforms reach back a long way to re-establish the Passover festival, celebrating the Israelites' rescue from Egypt, as commanded in the book of Deuteronomy. His actions were far-reaching: he removed pagan vessels from the temple, destroyed the high places and places of child sacrifice and took away the props for fertility worship. He did all this and more, while knowing that it would not avert judgement. Manasseh and the evil he did had put Judah on the path to destruction; the nation would be exiled. But Josiah was determined to make one last attempt to fulfil the covenant.

Josiah's was a faithfulness that did not depend on incentives. He pressed on, not because it would change anything but because he wanted to be obedient to God. As a Christian, what's in it for us? It is easy to follow God when life is good, when God answers our prayers and protects us from harm. It's not so easy when God makes difficult demands of us or things don't go our way. Will we follow God anyway?

Lord, help me to be faithful, even when the going gets hard. 'Trust and obey, for there's no other way to be happy in Jesus, but to trust and obey' (John Henry Sammis, 1846–1919).

ROSIE WARD

A glimmer of hope?

In the thirty-seventh year of the exile of King Jehoiachin of Judah, in the twelfth month, on the twenty-seventh day of the month, King Evil-merodach of Babylon, in the year that he began to reign, released King Jehoiachin of Judah from prison; he spoke kindly to him, and gave him a seat above the other seats of the kings who were with him in Babylon. So Jehoiachin put aside his prison clothes. Every day of his life he dined regularly in the king's presence. For his allowance, a regular allowance was given him by the king, a portion every day, as long as he lived.

What must it have been like? Thirty-seven years in captivity – and suddenly you are given a measure of freedom. This is a surprising end to a story of ever-deepening gloom. And it has prompted some debate: how should we respond to these final verses of 2 Kings?

Was this the end of Israel and Judah? Or is there a note of hope? There is still a 'king of Judah', so perhaps there is still a chance that all the promises about a king in David's line may be fulfilled, however unlikely it may look. This must surely have given the exiles a glimmer of hope through the long years.

I can remember a time when my life seemed very bleak. Everything I had hoped for and worked towards had crumbled away. My favourite prayer at the time came from Psalm 13:1: 'How long, O Lord?' Eventually an answer came from what seemed like nowhere. It was a link with the past, and it turned my default prayer to Psalm 30:5b: 'Weeping may linger for the night, but joy comes with the morning.' The night may be long, but morning will come.

Babylon was the place from which the return from exile and restoration of Jerusalem would begin. Jerusalem was rebuilt and, many years later, Jesus, a descendent of Jehoiachin (Matthew 1:12, Jechoniah), came. In our fragile world, when we face personal tragedy or global threats, knowing that ultimately we are safe in God's hands and that he has a plan to remake our world can give us hope.

'I know the plans I have for you… to give you a future with hope'
(Jeremiah 29:11).

ROSIE WARD

Judgement

What do you imagine when you think of the biblical concept of judgement? Do you feel anxious, envisioning yourself on the Day of Judgement being made to account for your life, or are you encouraged by thoughts of justice and fairness? You might remember Jesus talking about sheep and goats being sorted – the faithful welcomed into his kingdom and the selfish thrown into eternal punishment. Or you might recall examples in scripture of people being filled with God's wisdom and showing good judgement.

The first story in the Bible to involve humans is one in which God gives a judgement upon their behaviour. The last book in the Bible is an apocalyptic vision of God's judgement at the end of time. And the books between Genesis and Revelation are full of descriptions of judgement, and they are varied in their approach. We are reminded that making judgement is fraught with difficulty and should be carried out with the support of others. We hear of kings and beggars, patriarchs and prophets, young and old, all making decisions or taking actions that we – as readers – judge to be good or bad. We also come across people who are faced with the responsibility of pronouncing judgement upon others or who have God's judgement pronounced upon them. Each incident is often more complex than it might initially appear.

As we look at descriptions of judgement, keep in mind these questions:

- How do the main characters in this story feel about themselves? Does this affect the way in which they react to God?

- As we journey through the Bible, can we see a change over time in our understanding of God and judgement?

- Do we believe that judgement is principally about punishment or about guidance? Do our opinions affect how we read each story?

- Can we think of a time when we have felt judged or have passed judgement on another? Does that influence our interpretation of what is happening in these stories?

God never gives up on us. With God's help, we don't have to be afraid of judgement.

AMANDA BLOOR

The first judgement

She took of its fruit and ate; and she also gave some to her husband, who was with her, and he ate… Then the Lord God said, 'See, the man has become like one of us, knowing good and evil; and now, he might reach out his hand and take also from the tree of life, and eat, and live forever' – therefore the Lord God sent him forth from the garden of Eden, to till the ground from which he was taken.

There will be moments in our lives when our actions have long-lived and unforeseen consequences. Here, the first human couple deliberately ignore God's instruction and suffer the penalties of sin. Not only are they forced to leave the garden that has been their only home, but the pain of childbearing and the sweat of toil will be their lot and that of their descendants. They are judged to have chosen independence over obedience and must live with the results of their decision.

Although this is a story about sin and judgement, it is also a story that roots us to the earth. Adam and Eve have experienced abundance and luxuriant growth. The garden is full of everything that is pleasant to look at and good to eat. The first commandment of God to his human creations is to 'be fruitful' and to care for the earth and all that lives on it. The man and the woman look after the garden of Eden and continue that work after their expulsion, the difference being that the ground is now desolate, bringing forth thistles and thorns and requiring back-breaking effort to cultivate.

We also are tasked by God to care for the earth and all that lives on it; it's sadly easy to see the results of neglect or abuse of creation as nations suffer famine, lands become infertile and winds whip through deforested wastelands. What will future generations think of our carelessness and greed? What would God wish us to do in response?

Creator God, maker of heaven and earth, guide me today. Fill me with the desire to look after your wonderful creation, entrusted to us all. Amen

AMANDA BLOOR

Sharing the burden

When Moses' father-in-law saw all that he was doing for the people, he said, 'What is this that you are doing for the people? Why do you sit alone, while all the people stand around you from morning until evening?' Moses said to his father-in-law, 'Because the people come to me to inquire of God...' Moses' father-in-law said to him, 'What you are doing is not good. You will surely wear yourself out, both you and these people with you. For the task is too heavy for you; you cannot do it alone.'

It's often those who know us best who are able to say things we need to hear. In this passage, it's Moses' father-in-law who takes stock of the situation and realises that Moses is living with an unsustainable workload. His solution is simple: share the burden with a small, trustworthy group, so that Moses can stick to judging only the most important cases himself.

There have been many times when I've tried to do everything myself, believing that my vocation to ministry demands that I give all of myself and all my efforts to God's service. It's taken someone else to point out that I need help, that I'm beginning to get tired and to make mistakes or that, by reserving everything important into my own hands, I'm not allowing others to exercise their God-given gifts. It might have been hard to hear, but looking back I've been grateful to have been told this. I've tried to do the same for my own friends and colleagues.

Sometimes, when we want to do things well, we can become so focused on the major issue that we lose our sense of judgement. That's when the advice of others can be crucial. How might God speak to you through someone else today?

Lord, I want to do something good for you and to prove that I deserve your trust. But I know that sometimes I can take on more than I should. Help me to listen to guidance and to find ways of working with others to share the burden. Through Christ I pray. Amen

AMANDA BLOOR

Learning to trust

At that time Deborah, a prophetess, wife of Lappidoth, was judging Israel. She used to sit under the palm of Deborah between Ramah and Bethel in the hill country of Ephraim; and the Israelites came up to her for judgement. She sent and summoned Barak son of Abinoam from Kedesh in Naphtali, and said to him, 'The Lord, the God of Israel, commands you, "Go, take position at Mount Tabor, bringing ten thousand from the tribe of Naphtali and the tribe of Zebulun."'

The Old Testament is full of stories of kings and warriors, some of whom were good and trustworthy, while others were wicked, self-seeking or arrogant. It's not surprising, in a patriarchal society, that most were male. After all, if you were relying upon the ability to wield a sword or drive a chariot against your enemies, you'd look for strength as well as foresight. Yet in this passage, we see a woman, Deborah, described not just as a prophet but also as a leader who sits in judgement for the people of Israel. She must have been a well-respected figure, for she is able to order Barak, a senior military leader, to do what God was commanding through her: to take ten thousand warriors into battle against King Jabin's army.

It can be easy to pass judgement on others by what we see or expect. Barak was at first reluctant to trust Deborah's grasp of military strategy and had to learn to look beyond his own assumptions and prejudices. If we are honest with ourselves, we can probably think of times when we have found it hard to listen to guidance because of our preconceptions about the person delivering it. Just as Barak discovered that God truly could speak judgement by the mouth of a woman, so we might have to learn to look beyond the superficial and evaluate the message, rather than the messenger.

God of all wisdom, teach me today not to judge by outward appearances, but by what comes from the heart. Help me to listen to your message spoken by others, give me good discernment and help me to trust. Amen

AMANDA BLOOR

Pronouncing God's judgement

Then the Lord said to Samuel, 'See, I am about to do something in Israel that will make both ears of anyone who hears of it tingle. On that day I will fulfil against Eli all that I have spoken concerning his house, from beginning to end. For I have told him that I am about to punish his house forever, for the iniquity that he knew, because his sons were blaspheming God, and he did not restrain them.'

It is an awful responsibility to pass on bad news. It is difficult enough when you are speaking as one equal to another; it is almost impossible when there is a disparity in rank and age. This is the situation in which young Samuel finds himself. He is tasked with telling Eli that God's patience has run out and that judgement has been pronounced upon his entire family. It's a dreadful message to have to convey, but he does it with courage and obedience.

As a director of ordinands, I've helped people investigate what they believe is a calling to ordained ministry. After months – or years – of discernment, they submit themselves to the scrutiny of the church and wait anxiously for a decision. Many will have their vocation affirmed, but to some the church will say, 'This is not for you.' Having to telephone someone I've got to know very well and destroy their hopes is hard; it's a bitter blow to receive. But better that the news comes from me than from a stranger.

Eli listens to Samuel and knows that God's judgement is just. 'It is the Lord,' Eli says. 'Let him do what seems good to him.' I've found that many disappointed would-be clergy recognise over time that their calling does indeed lie elsewhere. There will be times in our lives when we have to say something that is hard for a friend or a loved one to hear. Do we have the courage to speak out?

Gracious God, help me not to be afraid to say what is necessary for others to hear. In difficult circumstances, give me the words I need to speak. Amen

AMANDA BLOOR

Good judgement

The king said, 'Divide the living boy in two; then give half to one, and half to the other.' But the woman whose son was alive said to the king – because compassion for her son burned within her – 'Please, my lord, give her the living boy; certainly do not kill him!' The other said, 'It shall be neither mine nor yours; divide it.' Then the king responded: 'Give the first woman the living boy; do not kill him. She is his mother.'

It's always seemed strange to me that this story, full of horror, grief and anger, is often taught to children. A dead baby, a mother so distraught by loss that she steals another woman's infant and a brutally pragmatic solution from the king to whom they appeal – 'Cut the baby in half, and give one piece to each woman.' Such brutality should surely be hidden from the young. But perhaps children are more robust than their elders, recognising that the world can be a frightening place where dreadful things happen, knowing that they are vulnerable and understanding that others hold power out of all proportion to their own agency. They also appreciate true maternal love, which would give up a child in order to protect it.

We can console ourselves with the distance of history: this must have been an empty threat. King Solomon surely wouldn't have done anything so horrible. But the truth is that the threat only worked because it was credible; the women knew that rulers could do anything and that the life of a baby born to people like them, on the fringes of society, was effectively worthless. Solomon's wisdom lay in understanding the realities of absolute authority and using them as the quickest way to cut through claim and counterclaim. Such wisdom was, in the eyes of his people, so far beyond normal understanding that it had to be God-given.

Each day we will be faced with decisions to be made and actions to be carried out. Pray that we are given the gift of God's wisdom to help us make good judgements.

Loving God, fill me with your Holy Spirit today and every day,
that I may act wisely and well. Amen

AMANDA BLOOR

Being thankful

For not from the east or from the west and not from the wilderness comes lifting up; but it is God who executes judgement, putting one down and lifting up another. For in the hand of the Lord there is a cup with foaming wine, well mixed; he will pour a draught from it, and all the wicked of the earth shall drain it down to the dregs. But I will rejoice forever; I will sing praises to the God of Jacob.

When we think of God's judgement, it's easy to feel like a small child being told off for bad behaviour and to become anxious or afraid. We are often our own worst critics, endlessly revisiting the things we are sorry for and wondering if God will truly forgive us. We can worry about what lies in store and focus only on regrets and mistakes. Yet God looks at the whole picture of our lives, not just part of it.

The book of Psalms is a wonderful treasury of human experience, containing songs that express the whole range of human emotion, from gratitude to anger and from joy to despair. While we tend to censor the language we use before God in prayer and worship, putting on a brave face and pretending that all is well, the psalmist is unafraid to say it as it is. God knows the secrets of our hearts anyway; why try to pretend otherwise?

In this particular psalm, the whole of God's judgement is examined in detail. There is a deep justice at the heart of God and the wicked will be forced to confront their deeds. But, as Jesus once reminded his listeners, how much does his Father long to give good things to his children? The psalmist recognises that God's judgement encompasses approval, 'lifting up' those who deserve encouragement and causing them to rejoice. 'I will sing praises,' says the psalmist, and 'rejoice forever'.

Take some time today to look at the things that you have thought, said and done. Be clear about the things that you got wrong and ask for forgiveness. But remember that God sees the good things too and wants to affirm them. Accept God's love for you and be thankful.

AMANDA BLOOR

Interpreting God's judgement

Daniel answered in the presence of the king, 'Let your gifts be for yourself, or give your rewards to someone else! Nevertheless, I will read the writing to the king and let him know the interpretation... This is the interpretation of the matter: MENE, God has numbered the days of your kingdom and brought it to an end; TEKEL, you have been weighed on the scales and found wanting; PERES, your kingdom is divided and given to the Medes and Persians.'

The story of Belshazzar's feast is a vivid illustration of how poor human judgement can bring about divine judgement. King Belshazzar, overcome by the illusions of power and wealth, behaves outrageously in front of the guests, who egg him on to blasphemous misuse of the holy vessels taken from the temple. Perhaps he imagines that riches and influence will shield him from the realities of life; his drunken debauchery simply reflects the unreality of the world he believes that he is living in.

The outbreak of the global Covid-19 pandemic last year was, perhaps, a wake-up call for us all, as it became clear that some things are completely beyond our control. Although the wealthy and privileged with large houses and gardens undoubtedly found it easier to self-isolate than those living in overcrowded or poor housing, the virus was no respecter of status or position. Rich and poor alike found themselves vulnerable to illness and facing the realities of human mortality. Some found their faith strengthened as they relied upon God, while others faced despair and loss.

In the Bible story, God breaks through to King Belshazzar in dramatic fashion, with judgement that is both accurate and inescapable. The illusory nature of worldly position and power is made clear as Belshazzar faces death rather than the glory he believed to be his right. Do we have the humility to recognise where true riches are to be found and that only God's kingdom is everlasting?

Great God, look gently upon me today. Help me to judge well in the choices I make, that I may follow Christ's example of self-sacrifice rather than seeking personal gain. Amen

AMANDA BLOOR

Things are not always as they seem

Now the birth of Jesus the Messiah took place in this way. When his mother Mary had been engaged to Joseph, but before they lived together, she was found to be with child from the Holy Spirit. Her husband Joseph, being a righteous man and unwilling to expose her to public disgrace, planned to dismiss her quietly. But just when he had resolved to do this, an angel of the Lord appeared to him in a dream.

There's a great deal of tenderness in this story. We can all feel for Joseph, 'a righteous man' who clearly loves his fiancée dearly and must be distressed beyond words to discover her pregnancy. Yet we all understand Mary's position too; she knows that she is without reproach and has not betrayed the man to whom she is promised. Her courage in saying 'yes' to God requires her not only to put her cares for herself aside, but also to trust that God will heal Joseph's broken heart.

Joseph, of course, judges Mary by what he knows to be commonplace. I wonder how he found out about the expected child, if Mary told him or if he noticed the signs. Perhaps one of Mary's household slipped a word in his ear. However he discovered the pregnancy, there was only one truth he could see: the woman he was preparing to spend the rest of his life with must have been unfaithful. His kindness in quietly setting her aside, instead of publicly denouncing her as an adulterer, does not detract at all from the hurt and disappointment he must have been feeling and the judgement he made.

God's angelic intervention in this story is a reminder that our knowledge is always partial; we never see the whole picture and cannot know what lies behind things that might at first glance appear clear-cut. We might have experienced the misunderstanding of others or have rushed into judging another with only sketchy information. Judgement is perilous and should always be reserved for God.

If you are tempted to judge someone for their behaviour today,
try to offer them in prayer before God instead. Pray for yourself, too!

AMANDA BLOOR

To save, not to condemn

'For God so loved the world that he gave his only Son, so that everyone who believes in him may not perish but may have eternal life. Indeed, God did not send the Son into the world to condemn the world, but in order that the world might be saved through him. Those who believe in him are not condemned; but those who do not believe are condemned already, because they have not believed in the name of the only Son of God. And this is the judgement, that the light has come into the world, and people loved darkness rather than light because their deeds were evil.'

Throughout our faith history, we can see evidence of God trying again and again to lead us into right ways of behaviour and of relationship. When we turn away, there is God, calling us back. Eventually, when humanity shows no sign of learning from previous mistakes, God makes the ultimate offer of restoration and salvation: Jesus Christ is sent into the world to bring light and hope.

This crucial passage from John's gospel gives us Jesus' own words. Having been questioned by Nicodemus, a seeker of the truth, Jesus explains how he understands the task ahead of him: he is to save the world rather than condemn it. It is no easy undertaking, of course, and there is an acknowledgement that not all people will listen to his message and change their ways. For those who are shown the light of truth but choose to hide in darkness and follow evil, there will be judgement. This is the reality of God's justice.

But there is great generosity too and a deep desire to save, even at huge cost. God knows the risk that is being taken by Jesus – that humanity will not listen and will turn in anger on the one who shines a spotlight on their wrongdoing – but that is a price worth paying. Jesus came to save, not condemn, so that those who believe might have eternal life.

Jesus, my Saviour, give me courage to step into the light and reveal to you those things that I have hidden in darkness. Save me from fear, help me to confess my sins and let me receive your forgiveness. Amen

AMANDA BLOOR

Be merciful

'If you love those who love you, what credit is that to you?… But love your enemies, do good and lend, expecting nothing in return. Your reward will be great, and you will be children of the Most High; for he is kind to the ungrateful and the wicked. Be merciful, just as your Father is merciful. Do not judge, and you will not be judged; do not condemn and you will not be condemned.'

It's sadly true that some people are harder for us to love than others. It's difficult to remain calm and measured when we feel under attack and when we're angry or disappointed; it's very easy to judge. Yet in Jesus' kingdom, everyone matters and all deserve mercy. It's a concept often summed up in the golden rule: do to others as you would have them do to you. Or, as here, do to others as you would have God do to you.

I can easily call to mind people and situations that have taken effort to forgive: the school bully; the male priest who refused to accept my ordination as valid; the work colleague who repeatedly undermined my efforts; the thief who stole from my housebound grandmother. I'm sure that each of us could compile a similar list. At the time, it was hard to keep a sense of balance or to look for reasons not to judge the offender. But looking back, I can begin to understand the hurt, exclusion, insecurity or damage that might have caused the behaviour.

We can easily make snap judgements about people and their actions, especially if we feel hurt, but we hope that God, faced with our failures, will be merciful and kind. We expect God to know us so well that we are not judged harshly. Jesus seems to be suggesting, in this passage, that we should act as God does, for only then can there be genuine mutuality and community. Do not judge, for then you will not be judged.

Ask God to help you look at your day and identify those times when you have passed judgement on others. Try to look on them with God's loving eyes and be kind.

AMANDA BLOOR

Bitter self-judgement

They went out to the Mount of Olives. And Jesus said to them, 'You will all become deserters; for it is written, "I will strike the shepherd, and the sheep will be scattered"'… Peter said to him, 'Even though all become deserters, I will not.' Jesus said to him, 'Truly I tell you, this day, this very night, before the cock crows twice, you will deny me three times.' But he said vehemently, 'Even though I must die with you, I will not deny you.'

When I was a child, I had a book of stories of the saints, most of whom came to sticky ends. I read with a mixture of emotions: admiration for their faith, dismay for the cruelty they suffered and certainty that I probably wouldn't be able to withstand torture and testing with such steadfastness.

In this passage, we see Peter failing to live up to his own expectations. Determined to be better than all the other disciples, when faced with the reality of denunciation and punishment, he crumbles. Peter, I think, carries this failure with him so that whatever he does afterwards is coloured by the bitter remembrance of betrayal. It's a hard burden to bear, and one that Jesus gently takes away after the resurrection, by allowing Peter to redeem himself – 'Do you love me? Feed my sheep' (see John 21:15–19).

We all want to do well for God, but we will all, at times, fail. There are examples throughout Christian history of people who have bravely endured terrible things, but for every Dietrich Bonhoeffer or Óscar Romero – to name just two recent martyrs – there will be many more who feel that they have let God down. I'm sure I'm not the only person to wake in the early hours, hot with shame as I remember actions or words I regret. Jesus understands; in this story, his loving judgement of Peter's actions is lighter than Peter's judgement of himself.

Lord, I know only too well that I fail you every day. I try, but then I stumble and fall. Do not judge me harshly, but trust me to do something for you, that I may redeem myself in my own eyes as well as yours. Amen

AMANDA BLOOR

Speaking judgement

'You stiff-necked people, uncircumcised in heart and ears, you are forever opposing the Holy Spirit, just as your ancestors used to do. Which of the prophets did your ancestors not persecute? They killed those who foretold the coming of the Righteous One, and now you have become his betrayers and murderers. You are the ones that received the law as ordained by angels, and yet you have not kept it.' When they heard these things, they became enraged.

When we hear uncomfortable truths about ourselves, we can respond in two ways: accept the justice behind the words and amend our ways, or furiously deny them. Stephen, the first Christian martyr, executed by stoning outside the walls of Jerusalem, knows that his accusers are potentially violent, but he speaks out anyway. Arrested on false charges, he pronounces judgement upon the city's religious leaders and is put to a cruel, though officially sanctioned, death.

We can probably all think of times when we've been criticised by others, sometimes unnecessarily harshly. It's something that has been thrown sharply into focus by electronic communication; the distancing effect of email and social media can mean that people are intemperate in their use of language and less kind than they might be face to face. Pointing out someone's faults is a delicate task if words are to be heard and acted upon, but there are times when ignoring an issue becomes impossible.

There's a deep irony in the fact that church communities, supposedly places of love and fellowship, can either become divided by the very public telling of uncomfortable truths or collude in covering up things that need to be addressed. It's not a new issue. Jesus advised his disciples that criticism of a church member was best done in private, then if necessary with one or two witnesses present. Only if the matter remained unresolved should it be taken to the whole church (Matthew 18:15–17). It's good advice.

What are the situations in your church, family or community that give you concern? How might you best raise them so that they are heard and not dismissed? Pray for God's guidance and wisdom.

AMANDA BLOOR

Judgement and grace

But the free gift is not like the trespass. For if the many died through the one man's trespass, much more surely have the grace of God and the free gift in the grace of the one man, Jesus Christ, abounded for the many. And the free gift is not like the effect of the one man's sin. For the judgement following one trespass brought condemnation, but the free gift following many trespasses brings justification.

Like all parish priests, I take a significant number of funerals each year. Usually they're moving and uplifting occasions; beneath the sorrow and grief lie lasting bonds of affection and love. Occasionally, though, a death reveals deep divisions within a family. It's heartbreaking to have to seat one set of mourners at a distance from another and harder still to discover siblings, children or partners who, because of the breakdown of relationships, refuse to attend the funeral of someone to whom they had once been close. Even the knowledge of mortality has not allowed reconciliation.

We began this series of studies by looking at the first judgement, the expulsion from Eden. Here, the apostle Paul contrasts that 'trespass' with the gift offered to humanity by Christ's self-giving on the cross. One man (Adam) set the whole world out of balance; one man (Jesus) puts the world back into right relationship with God. It's a gift that we can never hope to repay, but it gives us an example to follow.

I think, in my lifetime, of the fall of the Berlin Wall, the end of apartheid in South Africa and the establishment of the peace process in Northern Ireland. Political action had to be followed by the often-painful process of reconciliation between divided communities if a lasting peace was to be possible. If we are to live in harmony with each other, we need to set aside thoughts of bitterness and judgement in order, as Jesus showed, to forgive with boundless generosity.

Grace-filled God, generous Saviour, powerful Spirit, show me the parts of my life where reconciliation with you or others is necessary. Help me to forgive, to move forward and to rebuild. Amen

AMANDA BLOOR

After judgement comes the promise of life

Nothing accursed will be found there any more. But the throne of God and of the Lamb will be in it, and his servants will worship him; they will see his face, and his name will be on their foreheads. And there will be no more night; they need no light of lamp or sun, for the Lord God will be their light, and they will reign forever and ever.

Much of the faith history described in the Bible is a reminder of the darkness of our deeds, our fragility and our tendency towards sinfulness. Even after the resurrection of Christ, the world still hangs in balance; we are offered salvation but the choice remains ours, and some choose to ignore it. Here, in the final book of the Bible, Revelation, we are given a vision of what eternal life can be if we follow God's guiding and turn to Christ.

In mystical language, John describes the holy city, the new Jerusalem, God's dwelling-place and the seat of divine glory. This 'new heaven and new earth', where there is no sorrow or pain, is open to all who have gone through the last judgement, the 'saints' who have kept God's command-ments and held fast to faith in Jesus. As for the others, the sinners who refuse to repent, there is judgement and death.

None of us knows how long our life will be or when the moment of our death will arrive, although we do know that life will at some point come to an end. Although to some readers, the book of Revelation seems terrifying, I read it as an example of God's enduring mercy: sinners are given oppor-tunity after opportunity to change their ways, the dragon that symbolises evil is overcome and God delights in all who enter into the realm of light and glory. The judgement upon Adam and Eve was exile and sorrow, but this last judgement brings all the faithful home. Paradise is regained and God's love endures forever.

Imagine how it would feel to be called into God's holy city, bathed in light and love. Give thanks that God has offered us eternal life.

AMANDA BLOOR

Secrets and mysteries in Mark

 The Beatles' transatlantic hit 'Do You Want To Know a Secret?', released in 1963, asked a timeless, universal question guaranteed to attract attention. Human nature, our innate curiosity that prompts all forms of learning, loves to know a secret. Secrets are so much more interesting than facts.

Former US Secretary for Defence Donald Rumsfeld gave the world a brilliant brain teaser. At a press briefing in 2002, he said, 'There are known knowns; there are things we know we know. We also know there are known unknowns; that is to say we know there are some things we do not know. But there are also unknown unknowns – the ones we don't know we don't know.' Were these sentences gobbledygook? Take another look. They actually hold a profound truth. We know Jesus lived 2,000 years ago, but we accept we don't know everything – we don't even know what we don't know! There is so much of the social environment of the time, so much of the religious rules and important implications, so much we will never know that suddenly our 'knowledge' is pared down to a mere splinter.

Mark's gospel leaps from the page with breathless intensity. It's as though he fears time is running out, and he can't get his information down fast enough. Mark uses the Greek word for 'immediately', *eutheos*, 41 times, which adds pace to the narrative. We cannot be certain of the exact authorship or date of writing, but it rings with all the hallmarks of eyewitness authenticity. It is widely held to be the first documentation of Christ's ministry, death and resurrection at a time of escalating Roman persecution of the new Christians, both Jews and Gentiles, and it's quite possible Peter and Paul had already been martyred. This gospel may be the shortest, but it certainly packs a punch.

So let's uncover some of the clues over these next two weeks as we begin to recognise the brilliance of this gospel. Let's look at the anomalies and mysteries and work out how they relate to the religious and political landscape of the time. Veiled meanings of parables and miracles become clear in the light of Jesus' death and resurrection. And let's ask ourselves the question: who would risk persecution and death for a myth?

ELIZABETH RUNDLE

Good news!

The beginning of the good news about Jesus the Messiah, the Son of God, as it is written in Isaiah the prophet: 'I will send my messenger ahead of you, who will prepare your way' – 'a voice of one calling in the wilderness, "Prepare the way for the Lord, make straight paths for him."' And so John the Baptist appeared in the wilderness, preaching a baptism of repentance for the forgiveness of sins.

To sell a story, article or novel, the first sentence has to grab the reader's attention. Not only does the opening of Mark's gospel grab our attention, but it also stands out as one of the most amazing sentences of all time. No 'ifs' or 'buts', but a bold statement of the best news ever – about the Messiah, the Son of God: Jesus.

Perhaps the opening sentence is so familiar you've not really given it a second thought. Or maybe this is the first time you've isolated Mark's beginning from our Lord's teaching, miracles and parables. Why, then, when appetites are whetted to know more about this Jesus, does Mark immediately turn to John the Baptist?

Once past the hook of verse 1, the reader or listener has to follow the clues Mark gives as to Jesus' true identity. To unravel this mystery, we need to do the same.

Our 21st-century minds may consider John the Baptist a little eccentric, and tomorrow we'll take a closer look at why Mark brings John the Baptist into the picture so early, but today we focus on John's message. His major theme was repentance. Repentance, in biblical terms, means a complete turnaround, a change of heart, and specifically a return to God. This was no cosy address to religious respectability; John drove to the heart of Mosaic law. The crowd repented en masse and offered themselves for baptism, a very public symbol of a fresh start.

How many new beginnings have you tried, whether in career, relationships, country, church house group or Bible study? John prepared the people to meet God's Messiah.

Help me, Lord, to prepare each day as a new beginning. Amen

ELIZABETH RUNDLE

God's messenger

John wore clothing made of camel's hair, with a leather belt round his waist, and he ate locusts and wild honey. And this was his message: 'After me comes the one more powerful than I, the straps of whose sandals I am not worthy to stoop down and untie. I baptise you with water, but he will baptise you with the Holy Spirit.' At that time Jesus came from Nazareth in Galilee and was baptised by John in the Jordan. Just as Jesus was coming up out of the water, he saw heaven being torn open and the Spirit descending on him like a dove. And a voice came from heaven: 'You are my Son, whom I love; with you I am well pleased.' At once the Spirit sent him out into the wilderness.

What on earth was John wearing and eating? It is peculiar to us, but not to first-century Jews. Mark's clue is found in 2 Kings 1:8, which is a description of Elijah, the great prophet who was the forerunner of God's expected Messiah (Malachi 4:5), a prophecy to which Jesus himself alluded (Matthew 17:11–12). John the Baptist was the first piece in the messianic jigsaw puzzle.

On the face of it, it would seem totally unnecessary for Jesus, God's Son, to take part in a public display of repentance. For Jesus this was a turning point, a public acknowledgement of a new beginning. No longer the carpenter's son from Nazareth, but God's beloved Son, fired up for his mission.

Hebrew scripture, our Old Testament, has numerous accounts of God speaking to those he had specially chosen. Mark is using this scriptural basis to proclaim that Jesus has been anointed by God as both his king and his servant – compare Isaiah 42:1; 61:1. God's voice in scripture means his divine presence.

Before theological training, I went on retreat. I needed space to get my head around the implications of such a life change. The human Jesus needed space before the start of his ministry.

Today, Lord, I will make time to stop, be still and listen for your voice deep within my heart. Amen

ELIZABETH RUNDLE

Healing and wholeness

A man with leprosy came to him and begged him on his knees, 'If you are willing, you can make me clean.' Jesus was indignant. He reached out his hand and touched the man. 'I am willing,' he said. 'Be clean!' Immediately the leprosy left him and he was cleansed. Jesus sent him away at once with a strong warning: 'See that you don't tell this to anyone.'

Leprosy was one of the most feared and infectious diseases in the time of Jesus. Not only was it disfiguring and debilitating, but the onset of the disease also spelt social isolation, meaning loss of earnings, family life and dignity – totally life-changing for the sufferer. So in this cameo account, apart from the healing miracle, we have three unexpected aspects that at first sight don't fit our image of Jesus.

First, the poor, desperate man went against his social obligation by approaching Jesus.

Next, we have the startling record of Jesus' response. We need to recognise the use of language here – the original word, the translations and the way words mutate their meanings across time and culture. Many scholars prefer the phrase 'moved with pity' to 'indignant', and some believe 'moved with anger' is more accurate. It's impossible to rewind the scene, but somewhere among those words, we find our own attitude to tragedy, injustice and raw human need. From the intense emotion of that situation, Jesus acted with compassion and power.

Finally, imagine the joy and relief that would have washed over the man. Jesus had cleansed him, had given him back his place with family and friends. Jesus had restored his life. He must have been bursting to show and tell everyone in sight. Why, then, should Jesus want this cleansing kept secret? Would you have been able to keep such a miracle secret? But Jesus anticipated the overwhelming expectations people would place on him. He knew crowds would follow him, not for his teaching but for physical healing, while his message of salvation was through the people's changed, healed hearts and attitudes.

Lord Jesus, cleanse me from the infectious diseases of criticism, jealousy, anger and pride. Amen

ELIZABETH RUNDLE

Great expectations

Jesus withdrew with his disciples to the lake, and a large crowd from Galilee followed. When they heard all he was doing, many people came to him from Judea, Jerusalem, Idumea, and the regions across the Jordan and around Tyre and Sidon. Because of the crowd he told his disciples to have a small boat ready for him, to keep the people from crowding him. For he had healed many, so that those with diseases were pushing forward to touch him. Whenever the impure spirits saw him, they fell down before him and cried out, 'You are the Son of God.' But he gave them strict orders not to tell others about him.

It can be terrifying when enthusiastic crowds surge and you are in danger of being swept off your feet. We read of tragic incidences where people have been crushed to death, such is the force of a human tide. So it's not difficult to imagine the atmosphere surrounding Jesus. Jesus was the superstar of the moment, the celebrity everyone wanted to get near.

Well, not everyone. The Pharisees were plotting how to kill Jesus (3:6). Why should they connive to murder a man who 'went around doing good' (Acts 10:38)? That remains a pertinent question today, as Christians still face persecution and death.

Back to Jesus and the pressing crowd, Mark's brief description is not a million miles away from mass hysteria. Expectations and tempers would have been in the stratosphere. But this was not God's way. Jesus had been tested in the wilderness to perform crowd-pleasing stunts – to turn stones into bread and throw himself off the highest point of the temple (Matthew 4:1–7). The Son of God had not entered the world to please crowds, to be some kind of seven-day wonder. Jesus had entered the world to lead people back to God – in other words, to offer salvation.

Is that why he gave those 'strict orders'? Was Jesus defusing their physical expectations, which would inevitably have diluted their spiritual expectation? We were not there; we cannot be certain. Our questions remain unanswered and unanswerable. Heaven touches earth in mystery.

Lord, in all the situations I don't understand,
grant me your peace and compassion. Amen

ELIZABETH RUNDLE

Perseverance

When he was alone, the Twelve and the others around him asked him about the parables. He told them, 'The secret of the kingdom of God has been given to you. But to those on the outside everything is said in parables so that, "they may be ever seeing but never perceiving, and ever hearing but never understanding; otherwise they might turn and be forgiven!"' Then Jesus said to them, 'Don't you understand this parable? How then will you understand any parable?'

I love driving through the countryside when the fields have been ploughed and soil prepared to receive the next crop. Some fields almost glow with rich earth, while others look dry and stony even to my inexpert eye. The terrain in Galilee, through which our Lord Jesus walked, is both fertile and stony. It took hard work, diligence and perseverance to produce good harvests.

Rabbinical teaching was loaded with riddles, stories and parables. Jesus had just delivered the parable of the sower (Mark 4:2–8). Now, Mark allows us to eavesdrop as Jesus explained the great parable to his disciples in private. In doing so, Jesus said the disciples had been given 'the secret of the kingdom of God'. What did he mean by this?

Consider how often you have heard the parable of the sower. Passed down over the centuries, it's cosy and familiar to us. We have heard it before and so, with a hundred other responsibilities and routine tasks to think about, its message is soon crowded out from our minds. Similarly, for the people gathered around Jesus, their familiarity with the ordinary imagery he uses would have made its message easily lost to those with short attention spans or just looking for a good story.

In this way, the parable is not so much about the sower or the seed, but *all* about the soil. Just as Galilean soil took hard work to reap a good harvest, Jesus is saying that his teaching requires careful, prayerful attention. Jesus' message is hidden, or secret, to those who are looking for the new, the entertaining or the esoteric. Jesus' parables are vivid expressions of the ordinary, but within them are the paths to the deepest spiritual truth, paths found only by diligent application and perseverance.

Lord Jesus, may your Holy Spirit give me courage to persevere. Amen

ELIZABETH RUNDLE

Who is this?

A furious squall came up, and the waves broke over the boat, so that it was nearly swamped. Jesus was in the stern, sleeping on a cushion. The disciples woke him and said to him, 'Teacher, don't you care if we drown?' He got up, rebuked the wind and said to the waves, 'Quiet! Be still!' Then the wind died down and it was completely calm. He said to his disciples, 'Why are you so afraid? Do you still have no faith?' They were terrified and asked each other, 'Who is this? Even the wind and the waves obey him!'

Ask yourself, do you ever echo the disciples' question, 'Who is this?' Yesterday we looked at the power of parable to unlock the secrets of God's kingdom. Today, we move from parable to a creation miracle.

Human achievements are truly staggering and complex, yet the power of raw nature – wind, fire, flood, earthquake and storm – remains beyond our control. This we have in common with the terrified disciples, tossed by the storm and fearing for their lives. But perhaps where we differ in our modern discipleship is how we interpret the miraculous outcome of this story. We who live with a modern understanding of natural phenomena may miss the significance of Jesus' miracle here. For those men with Jesus, there was only one source of power over creation's raw elements – God. God created heaven and earth, the sea and the dry land. God created order out of chaos; as Psalm 89:9 states, 'You rule over the surging sea; when its waves mount up, you still them.' And again, in Psalm 107:29: 'He stilled the storm to a whisper; the waves of the sea were hushed.' Look again at those ancient words and imagine the disciples' quickened heartbeats. Who is this man you are reading about?

Mark 4 ends with this universal question: a direct question to the individual heart and soul. How would you answer? And can your answer allow Jesus to breathe his calm and peace into your day now?

'Breathe through the heats of our desire Thy coolness and Thy balm; let sense be dumb, let flesh retire; speak through the earthquake, wind, and fire, O still small voice of calm!' (John Greenleaf Whittier, 1807–92).

ELIZABETH RUNDLE

Restoration

Then Jesus left the vicinity of Tyre and went through Sidon, down to the Sea of Galilee and into the region of the Decapolis. There some people brought to him a man who was deaf and could hardly talk, and they begged Jesus to place his hand on him. After he took him aside, away from the crowd, Jesus put his fingers into the man's ears. Then he spat and touched the man's tongue. He looked up to heaven and with a deep sigh said to him, *'Ephphatha!'* (which means, 'Be opened!'). At this, the man's ears were opened, his tongue was loosed and he began to speak plainly. Jesus commanded them not to tell anyone.

Verse 31 throws out an immediate puzzle. It reminds me of the old joke when a man asks for directions and the reply comes back, 'If I was going there, I wouldn't start from here.' Jesus was making his way south to the Galilee region by walking 22 miles north!

In contrast to the scant details of his journey south, Mark then goes into specific detail of the deaf man's healing. The symbolism in the detail would have been quickly understood in the first century. People thought that demons bound up ears and tongues, and Mark was demonstrating Jesus' power over evil. I find it fascinating that the healing properties of human saliva are the subject of current medical research. Jesus 'looked up to heaven', which was a sure sign that the power to heal came from God.

Mark writes the word *Ephphatha*, one of the few Aramaic words in the New Testament. Through this word, like the word *Abba*, we have an intimate sound of Jesus' own voice. The mysterious core of this miracle recalled the words of the prophet Isaiah in describing the new creation when Israel would be redeemed: 'Then will the eyes of the blind be opened and the ears of the deaf unstopped' (Isaiah 35:5). This miracle was a symbolic proclamation that Jesus was God's Messiah.

Yet Jesus 'commanded' them to silence. Inexplicable? In Mark 6, you'll find the reason for secrecy: John the Baptist had been beheaded, a foretaste of Jesus' own fate.

Thank you, Lord, for the precious gifts of sight, hearing,
speech, taste and touch. Amen

ELIZABETH RUNDLE

'What about you?'

Jesus and his disciples went on to the villages around Caesarea Philippi. On the way he asked them, 'Who do people say I am?' They replied, 'Some say John the Baptist; others say Elijah; and still others, one of the prophets.' 'But what about you?' he asked. 'Who do you say I am?' Peter answered, 'You are the Messiah.' Jesus warned them not to tell anyone about him.

How perplexing is this? When you have some fantastic news – you've passed an exam, got engaged, bought a new home, held your first child or grandchild – it's only natural to tell people. Peter declared the most significant news in Jewish history: his master, Jesus of Nazareth, is the Messiah! Is it credible that Jesus told them to keep quiet about it? On the surface, it makes no sense at all.

For hundreds of years the people of Israel had longed for the Messiah, God's anointed one. The greatest holy men of Israel had prophesied that the Messiah's arrival would change everything. But, like so many things we eagerly look forward to, when it actually happened, Israel was unprepared. That Jesus could be the Messiah came as a surprise, even a shock.

I guess more people have passed an opinion on Jesus than on any other figure in history. Like the disciples, we still seek other people's impressions and descriptions of people. But these verses make clear that Jesus was not interested in rumour, gossip or public opinion; he directly questioned each disciple. Pause for a moment and ask yourself, what is your impression of Jesus? Who would you say he is? I doubt if Peter knew exactly what he meant by his outburst, but his reverential devotion in that moment was absolute.

With evangelic fervour, Mark wrote to strengthen and encourage new Christians, both Jewish and Gentile. Peter's God-given flash of insight was not lost. Neither are your moments of vision and devotion. Cling on to them, for, like it did with Peter, 'stuff' will happen; as time went on, Peter's faith knew no bounds.

Lord Jesus Christ, so root me in your love that I may know myself
held in the mystery of your living presence. Amen

ELIZABETH RUNDLE

Transfiguration

After six days Jesus took Peter, James and John with him and led them up a high mountain, where they were all alone. There he was transfigured before them. His clothes became dazzling white, whiter than anyone in the world could bleach them. And there appeared before them Elijah and Moses, who were talking with Jesus… Suddenly, when they looked around, they no longer saw anyone with them except Jesus. As they were coming down the mountain, Jesus gave them orders not to tell anyone what they had seen until the Son of Man had risen from the dead. They kept the matter to themselves, discussing what 'rising from the dead' meant.

When we look in detail at Mark's gospel, so much is shrouded in mystery. Time and again this gospel, which pulses with such energy and purpose, confronts us with ambiguity. What connections can we make with this awesome episode to reveal the living Lord God to our own hearts and minds?

Let's think of the scripture Peter, James and John would have known. The pivotal moment in Israel's history was the exodus from Egypt. Moses had met God on Mount Sinai to receive the law; now here was Jesus on another 'high mountain'. Moses' encounter with God radiated from his face (Exodus 34:30). His closeness to God transformed him into Israel's great lawgiver and redeemer. Is Mark's account of a radiant, dazzling Jesus his way of telling the world that God's beloved Son has come to fulfil Mosaic law with God's law of inclusive love?

The other week my local church hosted an afternoon cafe worship entitled 'Let's talk about death'. Just like Peter, James and John, we had a deep discussion on the meaning of 'rising from the dead'. We also found ourselves perplexed, fearful, confused and of varied experience and expectation. Nevertheless, we were at one in believing in the same Jesus Christ, present with us now and present with us in the transforming future prepared for us.

Lord Jesus, show me that I can no more look at you as look into the sun, but that your love, like the sun, transforms my grey shadows into warm colours of love.

ELIZABETH RUNDLE

Palm Sunday

When they brought the colt to Jesus and threw their cloaks over it, he sat on it. Many people spread their cloaks on the road, while others spread branches they had cut in the fields. Those who went ahead and those who followed shouted, 'Hosanna!' 'Blessed is he who comes in the name of the Lord!' 'Blessed is the coming kingdom of our father David!' 'Hosanna in the highest heaven!' Jesus entered Jerusalem and went into the temple courts. He looked around at everything, but since it was already late, he went out to Bethany with the Twelve.

In first-century Palestine, the Jews had been without a king for well over 600 years until the Roman emperor appointed a puppet-king in Judea to subdue and control the population. Cue: Herod the Great. Herod's prodigious building programme was indeed 'great', but he was not 'of David's line'.

Prophets like Isaiah, Micah and Zechariah had given the people a longing and a vision for a just and powerful king, one who would save them from hated oppressors. That king would bring in God's rule of peace and prosperity. Pilgrims who travelled to the temple in Jerusalem were greeted by priests with words from Psalm 118:26–27: 'Blessed is he who comes in the name of the Lord… With boughs in hand, join in the festal procession.' And Jesus also knew how Zechariah had envisioned Zion's king: 'See, your king comes to you… lowly and riding on a donkey' (Zechariah 9:9).

When Jesus entered Jerusalem that day, he entered not as a warrior-king on a horse, encouraging a revolt, but on an animal of service and peace. It was a visual messianic statement. What a glorious, heady sight, the noise and expectation of the crowd rising ever higher as they approached the city walls and the temple! And then? Mark, the master of detail and suspense, comes to a halt. All the build-up, then nothing. Jesus just goes back to Bethany. The disciples must have been mystified. Only in hindsight is the true significance of that day appreciated. Jesus is no king of force, but of forgiveness, a suffering servant whose reign turns the world's values upside down. His is the new kingdom of God.

Lord, strengthen me to work for your kingdom of justice and peace.

ELIZABETH RUNDLE

Challenge

They arrived again in Jerusalem, and while Jesus was walking in the temple courts, the chief priests, the teachers of the law and the elders came to him. 'By what authority are you doing these things?' they asked... Jesus replied, 'I will ask you one question. Answer me, and I will tell you by what authority I am doing these things. John's baptism – was it from heaven, or of human origin? Tell me!' They discussed it among themselves and said, 'If we say, "From heaven," he will ask, "Then why didn't you believe him?" But if we say, "Of human origin"...' (They feared the people, for everyone held that John really was a prophet.) So they answered Jesus, 'We don't know.'

Rabbinical teaching in riddles was not to obscure truth but to prompt listeners to work out truth for themselves. Jesus, who had conspicuously ridden into Jerusalem with a rapturous crowd, had just angrily routed the money changers and stallholders from the temple. These actions, and perhaps many more unrecorded events, had aroused fury among Sanhedrin members, the chief priests, teachers of the law and elders – a powerful group to challenge.

Jesus replied to their question with a perfect question of his own. It takes us back to John the Baptist. Perhaps we do not pay enough attention to the symbolism of John. It's easy to forget John in the roller coaster of events leading to Jesus' arrest, but this incident makes it clear how important John had been in Jesus' eyes and in the hearts of those who had received baptism from him. Dipping into Matthew's gospel, we find that Jesus himself gave John the greatest accolade: 'Truly I tell you, among those born of women there has not risen anyone greater than John the Baptist' (Matthew 11:11).

So those learned men squirmed, falling back on the lamest of excuses, 'We don't know.' I can't help wondering if Nicodemus was one of those shadowy religious leaders, aghast but fascinated by the actions and teaching of this young man. If Nicodemus *was* present, and it's more probable than not, what a miracle took place in his heart following the crucifixion!

Lord, open my eyes to the dangers of self-satisfaction and insularity. Amen

ELIZABETH RUNDLE

Questions

Very early in the morning, the chief priests, with the elders, the teachers of the law and the whole Sanhedrin, made their plans. So they bound Jesus, led him away and handed him over to Pilate. 'Are you the king of the Jews?' asked Pilate. 'You have said so,' Jesus replied. The chief priests accused him of many things. So again Pilate asked him, 'Aren't you going to answer? See how many things they are accusing you of.' But Jesus still made no reply, and Pilate was amazed. Now it was the custom at the festival to release a prisoner whom the people requested… Wanting to satisfy the crowd, Pilate released Barabbas to them. He had Jesus flogged, and handed him over to be crucified.

Imagine that you are hearing this story for the first time. You follow Jesus' life and ministry as he travels from Galilee up to Jerusalem. Awesome miracles, radical and inspiring teaching – surely he is the Son of God! Excited crowds shouting 'Hosanna', the cry of 'Lord, save us!', are fresh in your mind.

Then you hear Jesus has been betrayed, arrested and brought before the hated Roman governor. You are confused. You follow as Pilate asks Jesus if he is the king of the Jews. Your hope is restored. But when you hear Jesus has been flogged, that terrible beating with metal-tipped thongs of leather that could kill weaker men, your heart races in desperation. Why was Jesus silent? It doesn't make sense for Pilate to hand over this good man to the excruciating public agony of crucifixion. You are devastated.

As Mark's gospel draws towards the end, everything seems to be falling apart. It doesn't make sense. Is this why the apostle Paul wrote to the first Christian believers in Corinth, 'For the message of the cross is foolishness to those who are perishing, but to us who are being saved it is the power of God' (1 Corinthians 1:18)? There is no secret or mystery to those who accept Jesus as God's Messiah. The victory of the cross is revealed in the eternal power of sacrificial love.

Lord of life and love, Lord of pain and glory, hear my prayers. Amen

ELIZABETH RUNDLE

The suffering servant

'Let this Messiah, this king of Israel, come down now from the cross, that we may see and believe.' Those crucified with him also heaped insults on him. At noon, darkness came over the whole land until three in the afternoon. And at three in the afternoon Jesus cried out in a loud voice, *'Eloi, Eloi, lema sabachthani?'* (which means 'My God, my God, why have you forsaken me'?). When some of those standing near heard this, they said, 'Listen, he's calling Elijah.' Someone ran, filled a sponge with wine vinegar, put it on a staff, and offered it to Jesus to drink. 'Now leave him alone. Let's see if Elijah comes to take him down,' he said. With a loud cry, Jesus breathed his last. The curtain of the temple was torn in two from top to bottom. And when the centurion, who stood there in front of Jesus, saw how he died, he said, 'Surely this man was the Son of God!'

A man hangs bleeding and, near to death, yells out as weakness and suffocation take their toll. Chief priests and teachers of the law taunt him with insults. 'Someone' offers the standard drink given to victims to deaden their pain. Darkness. The very word spreads a pall of sadness on a scene of intense heartbreak. The heartbreak of abandonment, a crystallised fragment of history which finds echoes in every violent, tragic death. A human scene over which, in every age, people have pondered, argued and gasped in wonder. The paradox of agony and hope. The death which would change the world.

But the centurion, a battle-hardened Roman soldier, used to watching enemies crucified, saw something unique in Jesus' death. God's suffering servant was recognised not by one of Jesus' followers, but by a foreigner. I think we can be certain his life changed from that moment, and non-Jewish readers would not miss the fact that a Gentile was the first 'convert' to emerging Christianity. A momentous declaration by a man who was there, how does this centurion's testimony challenge you?

'When I survey the wondrous cross… Love so amazing, so divine, demands my life, my soul, my all' (Isaac Watts, 1674–1748).

ELIZABETH RUNDLE

The end or the beginning?

As they entered the tomb, they saw a young man dressed in a white robe sitting on the right side, and they were alarmed. 'Don't be alarmed,' he said. 'You are looking for Jesus the Nazarene, who was crucified. He has risen! He is not here. See the place where they laid him. But go, tell his disciples and Peter, "He is going ahead of you into Galilee. There you will see him, just as he told you."' Trembling and bewildered, the women went out and fled from the tomb. They said nothing to anyone, because they were afraid.

If this was the end of Mark's 'good news about Jesus the Messiah, the Son of God' (1:1), it's no surprise that it has been called 'the greatest of all literary mysteries'. So much detail: we feel the creeping warmth of sunrise and the women's tense anxiety as they wonder what they will find. Jesus is gone. They run away. Anticipation and promise end abruptly in disappointment. Was Mark's original ending lost? Was the writer suddenly arrested and killed before his intended conclusion? Or does this gospel end with a stroke of genius, provoking those who read or hear it to want to know more?

Let's take a deeper look for the essence of these verses. Mark's message is loud and clear for all the world: 'He is not here.' By his resurrection, Jesus Christ has broken the boundaries of human understanding. We can no more understand this miracle than those terrified women who ran from the tomb. But what I find so truly wonderful is the fact that out of such mystified fear a Christian community has spread throughout all ages and now throughout the world. Yes, there is still persecution; yes, there is still apathy. But also, in every generation, there are those guiding saints who love and nurture us, enabling us to make our own leap of faith from the Jesus of history to accepting the living Lord into our lives. To quote the late biblical scholar William Barclay in his *Daily Study Bible*, 'Jesus is not a memory but a presence.'

Thanks be to God for the mystery and miracle of faith. Amen

ELIZABETH RUNDLE

Growing old

 The next two weeks offer reflections on the theme of ageing and growing old. There is no blueprint for this, nor does the Bible offer precise guidance. The Bible passages are drawn from a variety of contexts and their insights are not just for the later stages of life – growing is a task through all of life. The way we respond to what each stage of life brings prepares and resources us for the next – and particularly for the challenge of our final years. So, although these reflections focus particularly on the later stage of life, they are relevant for all readers, whatever your age.

In the Bible, the later years are a time of life to be honoured and reverenced. They are also where valuable gifts of lived experience and wisdom are to be found. Both are too easily forgotten in our day. It was said of a former prime minister that he was stepping down at precisely the moment when his experience meant he had the most to offer. The older years are similar. We may feel we have a lot to offer but nowhere to offer it. Above all, these years reveal God's faithfulness and constancy. 'I will be your God throughout your lifetime – until your hair is white with age. I made you, and I will care for you. I will carry you along and save you' (Isaiah 46:4, NLT).

But the vulnerability of life is never far away either. The prayers of those in their older years are a repeated theme in the Bible: 'Do not cast me away when I am old,' prays the psalmist. 'Do not forsake me when my strength is gone' (Psalm 71:9, NIV). Even in a world with pensions, social care and health provision, the vulnerability is never far away.

Wherever these reflections find us in life, may they strengthen faith, build hope and renew a sense of God's presence with us.

DAVID RUNCORN

Growing

Listen to me, O house of Jacob, all the remnant of the house of Israel, who have been borne by me from your birth, carried from the womb; even to your old age I am he, even when you turn grey I will carry you. I have made, and I will bear; I will carry and will save.

We start ageing from the moment we are born. We call it 'growing' at that point – which sounds more positive! It is unfortunate that we call the later stages of life 'ageing', as if 'growing' has stopped and declining has begun. In fact, there is no stage of life that does not involve growing. Our growing is never finished.

We call the first stage 'growing up'. The tasks in this stage involve the establishing of life, home, work and relationships. Though this never completely stops, the focus does begin to shift as we move into the second half, and later stages, of life. There is good reason why those years, in traditional cultures, are expected to prioritise the more inward qualities of reflection and contemplation. The focus is no longer so much on what we have achieved, but on its significance and meaning – not so much the container but what it contains. We reflect not only on what we have been doing but also on what kind of person we have become in the process.

Growing old is a challenge to be embraced as adventurously as growing up. As in all life, there will be losses and gains. Energies and priorities will change, for, as Carl Jung said, 'We cannot live in the afternoon of life according to the programme of life's morning.'

What stage of life are you living in? What does the invitation and challenge to be growing ask of you? In a well-known quote, attributed to Dom Hélder Câmara, a very old tree speaks of the challenge of growing throughout life and beyond: 'I love looking at you, hundred-year-old tree, loaded with shoots and boughs as though you were a stripling. Teach me the secret of growing old like you, open to life, to youth, to dreams, as somebody aware that youth and age are merely steps towards eternity.'

Lord, may I never stop growing. Amen

DAVID RUNCORN

Faith and fear

Do not fear, for I have redeemed you; I have called you by name, you are mine. When you pass through the waters, I will be with you; and through the rivers, they shall not overwhelm you; when you walk through fire you shall not be burned, and the flame shall not consume you. For I am the Lord your God, the Holy One of Israel, your Saviour.

Life, like faith, rarely happens in ideal circumstances. For all the gifts of life's later years, they bring particular and varied vulnerabilities – though these are not wholly unexpected. But the sudden arrival of Covid-19 has added a very particular threat to our world – and particularly to the older generations within it. It is a genuinely frightening time.

Many talks and sermons have stressed living by 'faith not fear', but I have never found it to be a straightforward exchange like that. Rather, our fears and anxieties are more like places of painful and tender bruising or cuts in our lives. There are reasons why we hurt as we do.

It may be more helpful to think of our fears as reflexes that need to be lovingly managed rather than being told to go away. Faith needs to speak into those places that are vulnerable within us, places where we feel our lack of strength and confidence. This is particularly true in times like these. Rather than a weakness, our fears might be thought of as wounds that do not heal quickly or easily. They are vulnerable to the bumps and knocks of life, and they easily get inflamed and infected again. Faith is the work of tenderly and patiently cleansing, soothing and rebinding those places within.

When we speak in faith to our fears, we are not telling them off. Rather it is a work of loving challenge, reminding all that is fragile within of God's steady, unchanging love and promises. So living by faith in a time of fear is a kind of physiotherapy. We apply our faith to those parts of us that need particular building up, working on the muscle and tissue that have been hurt or just unused. As we bind our anxieties and fears in faith, we are strengthened and enabled to be all we are intended to be in demanding times.

In loving faith, I name and bind up my fears this day.

DAVID RUNCORN

Times and seasons

For everything there is a season, and a time for every matter under heaven: a time to be born, and a time to die; a time to plant, and a time to pluck up what is planted; a time to kill, and a time to heal; a time to break down, and a time to build up; a time to weep, and a time to laugh; a time to mourn, and a time to dance... I have seen the business that God has given to everyone to be busy with. He has made everything suitable for its time.

The yearly round of creation is divided into seasons. In the western world, there are four – autumn, winter, summer and spring. Each has its own features, moods and character. Do you have a favourite? Which season are you most drawn to and can you say why?

And do you ever wonder if, for example, winter looks at summer's vibrant colour and warmth and feels guilty for its cold and lethargy? Does autumn envy the vigorous, youthful energy and life of spring? In fact, each season has its own gift and task without which the others cannot fulfil theirs. Each has a vital part to play, even if it is sometimes hard to appreciate. For everything there is a season. No season is more valuable than any other.

Like the rest of creation, human life has its seasons. These include the more predictable stages of life. But we might also notice how many events and happenings on that long list in today's passage are times we would not choose for ourselves. Not all are welcome or good news; some come as a surprise or shock. But each offers its gifts and challenges, has its beauty, leaves its scars, brings joys and pains, sets limits and opens possibilities.

How would you describe the season of your life at this time? What, within it, are you enjoying and celebrating? Perhaps it comes with things that are difficult to live with. Where are the gifts and the challenges of this season? Are there things to embrace and to value – even if it is tough going? For everything there is a season. And God is present in it all – seen and unseen.

Creator God, may I embrace everything in its time
and learn to find your presence there. Amen

DAVID RUNCORN

Remember you are dust (1)

Bless the Lord, O my soul… For he knows how we were made; he remembers that we are dust. As for mortals, their days are like grass; they flourish like a flower of the field; for the wind passes over it, and it is gone, and its place knows it no more. But the steadfast love of the Lord is from everlasting to everlasting on those who fear him.

'Remember that you are dust and to dust you shall return.' Those words are spoken at Ash Wednesday services as the sign of the cross is marked in ash on our foreheads.

And what exactly are we called to remember? Dust reminds us of our origins. The first human being, Adam, was made from the dust. The words speak not only of our origins but also our endings. What began as dust will return to dust. Like the grass of the fields and flowers in my garden, my life is a brief, passing thing. It may be that our perennial capacity for messing up, our misguided priorities and assumptions about who we are, lie in an unwillingness to live with this truth. Remembering all this keeps us honest and down to earth.

If we are but dust, what may we hope for? Who makes anything of dust? God does: 'He knows… he remembers that we are dust.' But this does not seem to frustrate God. Quite the reverse. It seems to inspire him! He chooses dust to be the prime ingredient for his crowning work in creation – a creature who bears his image. Shaped out of barren ground, the first creature of dust became a living being when God breathed into his nostrils (Genesis 2:7).

So here I am too, a dust creature, yet alive in the very breath of God's own being. My life is not my own. It is given to me – a gift of the most personal and intimate kind. God has written in the dust of our human nature the words of eternal life.

Find a dusty surface and write a prayer with your finger in the dust.
Thank God that he creates out of dust.

DAVID RUNCORN

Remember you are dust (2)

Bless the Lord, O my soul… For he knows how we were made; he remembers that we are dust. As for mortals, their days are like grass; they flourish like a flower of the field; for the wind passes over it, and it is gone, and its place knows it no more. But the steadfast love of the Lord is from everlasting to everlasting on those who fear him.

Yesterday we remembered the dust of our human origins. We come from the dust of the earth. We are mortal and finite. But we also remembered what God creates with dust. We are part of something much greater.

So dust I may be, but I am restless dust. I am dust that prays, loves, worships and hopes. There is a life stirring within me that is not my own. Deep down I know I am part of something much greater. An improbable story of life, wonder and mystery stirs within me. It is renewed in me with every breath I take. It may deepen with the years. I am dust with dreams of glory, of a life that is not yet my own and that I can barely imagine.

From childhood onwards so many of our stories echo this – stories of lives trapped, disfigured, lost or unvalued but that are really beautiful and beloved, all waiting for the kiss of one whose love is true to release the spells and reveal them for who they truly are. The ugly duckling is a majestic swan; the scullery maid is really the king's true love; the toad is a handsome prince. Dust I may be, but I am desired dust, beloved dust, dust with a destiny.

My deepest struggle may not, after all, be with my sin and waywardness (though these are real). It may instead lie in accepting the extraordinary love with which God chooses to love me in all my dustiness and in trusting what he will yet reveal of who I truly am in his sight.

Return to the dust-prayer you wrote yesterday. Imagine that God has written a reply to it. What might it be?

DAVID RUNCORN

Here I am

Samuel was lying down in the temple of the Lord, where the ark of God was. Then the Lord called, 'Samuel! Samuel!' and he said, 'Here I am!'

This is a key moment early in the long saga told in the books of 1 and 2 Samuel. A young boy who will become a great leader and prophet is lying in the temple, and God calls him: 'Samuel!' This happens four times because Samuel does not know yet who is speaking to him. Each time, however, he replies, 'Here I am.' In Hebrew storytelling, the first words a person speaks define their character and calling. Samuel, all his life, will be utterly present to God and his people.

To say 'Here I am' is not as easy as it sounds. We can, and often do, spend a great deal of our lives wishing we were someone else or somewhere else. The present can often simply be the place we would rather not be. This is especially true if we are in hard or painful places.

In his book *In the Shelter: Finding a home in the world*, Pádraig Ó Tuama shares his personal stories of life and faith. Like our own, they are a mixture of joy and pain, but I love his habit of greeting wherever he finds himself. Chapters telling of struggle finish with 'Hello to pain'. Times of confusion are greeted 'Hello to perplexity'. Any and everything is for greeting – anger, tears, the rain, the washing-up, the bad back. The wisdom of this habit is that it helps us to be present and to acknowledge what is here with us. God, who is always present ('I am'), cannot meet us where we are not or if we are trying to be someone we are not. 'Hello to trying to escape from here.'

So who, and what, in your world is present to greet today? Just say hello. 'Hello to here' and all that it contains. It is the only place to start. And as it is where God is to be found, it is the best place to start.

Hello to here. Hello to Jesus. Hello to what will be.

DAVID RUNCORN

Being led

When they had finished breakfast, Jesus said to Simon Peter… 'Very truly, I tell you, when you were younger, you used to fasten your own belt and to go wherever you wished. But when you grow old, you will stretch out your hands, and someone else will fasten a belt around you and take you where you do not wish to go… Follow me.'

In their original context these words foretold Peter's future imprisonment and martyrdom for Christ. But they describe very well a particular experience of the later years of life (but also perhaps earlier). With ageing there is a steady, and sometimes sudden, loss of freedom. We simply cannot do what we used to. We must rely, increasingly, on the help and support of others. The reasons will be varied – health, strength, mobility, finances (our own and those we share life with). Whatever the cause, it is not the way we would wish things to be.

As we are part of a society that greatly prizes independence, it is possible we may not have learned any other way of living and valuing ourselves. We know ourselves in giving and being useful. But here we are, whatever the reason, having to 'stretch out our hands' and let others give to us. This loss of independence in its various forms is very tough. It can feel humiliating. One person called it 'harrowing'. We may fear being a burden on others. This is a way we 'do not wish to go'.

This is not easy to write about because no two stories are alike. Nor should we minimise the isolation of those times when the care and support we need is just not there. But a key quality of Christian loving and living is best described as interdependence. It is known in a mutuality of giving and receiving. We may need gently, steadily, to be reminded that there is dignity in receiving as well as in giving. There is humility in knocking and asking for what we need – sometimes others simply do not know. There is grace in being loved as well as loving. The call is still 'Follow me'.

Lord, help me to go where I would not choose and to allow myself to receive where once I always gave. Amen

DAVID RUNCORN

Waiting

**His divine power has given us everything needed for life and godliness...
For this very reason, you must make every effort to support your faith
with goodness, and goodness with knowledge, and knowledge with
self-control, and self-control with endurance, and endurance with godliness, and godliness with mutual affection, and mutual affection with
love. For if these things are yours and are increasing among you, they
keep you from being ineffective and unfruitful in the knowledge of our
Lord Jesus Christ.**

The remarkably rapid spread of the Christian faith in the first few centuries
is easily assumed to be the outcome of bold, confident faith. We miss just
how often the New Testament letters remind believers to live with patience,
endurance and perseverance (for example, Hebrews 10:36; Colossians
1:11; Romans 12:12). This suggests that the reality was rather different
from constant success stories. It also means there is an important place for
discipleship that cannot be measured in terms of immediate, visible results.

Our culture has no positive use for patience and waiting, so we do not
come to this insight easily. Everything is focused on doing – and doing it
ever faster. But this waiting and patience is not passive. It is not simply
what we do at bus stops. Faithful waiting is poised and watchful. On the
sports field, waiting is the skill that makes the moment to move decisive
and game changing. A waiter in a restaurant is highly alert and ready to
respond at need or signal. Faithful waiting is a work of active participation.

Donald Eadie has lived for years with chronic physical disability. He
writes of needing a different kind of waiting that cannot be tied to time or
preferred outcomes. It has to be trusting and open-ended. He calls this a
'waiting beyond the waiting'. It means losing control. It asks for a surrender
and a willingness to be shaped by 'something that is far beyond our own
imaginings'. In the later, often less active, stages of life, this kind of waiting
and patience can be a central feature of faithful living. It is not easy, but
through it we are formed. It becomes a gift.

---

*Lord, when life needs it most, help me to wait in patience
beyond all my preferred outcomes. Amen*

DAVID RUNCORN

God has made me bitter

'Call me no longer Naomi [Pleasant], call me Mara [Bitter], for the Almighty has dealt bitterly with me. I went away full, but the Lord has brought me back empty; why call me Naomi when the Lord has dealt harshly with me, and the Almighty has brought calamity upon me?'

Naomi's life has been a series of tragedies and losses in exile. As she returns at last to her hometown, her restraint gives way. Anger and pain pour out. It is God she blames. This is recorded without rebuke or correction. Her business is with God.

The freedom to protest, to be angry and to complain to God is a feature of biblical faith. From the greatest leaders, teachers and prophets to a widowed refugee called Naomi, all must raise their voice. To question and challenge God's absence in times of crisis, or the apparent injustice of his actions, is a legitimate act of faith – not a lack of it. And God does not require our prayers to be polite!

Two-thirds of the psalms begin from places of lament and protest. They are full of urgent questioning and impatient petition: 'Answer me when I call, O God!' (Psalm 4:1); 'Why, O Lord do you stand far off?' (Psalm 10:1); 'Rise up, O Lord… do not forget the oppressed' (Psalm 10:12).

By contrast, lament is largely absent from the prayers and songs of modern Christian worship. This leaves us with no language for the times when life hits us hard or seems unfair and when God seems to let us down. We may even judge ourselves for feeling angry with God. Where there is no place for lament, people will suffer in silence. Stories will go untold. Naomi teaches us a different way. Lament keeps our worship and prayers honest. It refuses to allow religion to be a spiritual escape from the painful contradictions of a real world.

Are there times you have felt like Naomi? Can you bring your pain to God as she does? A great gift at such times are those friends with whom we do not have to pretend either.

'Dear God, this is honestly how I am feeling about you and about life…'
If this is appropriate to you, how might that prayer continue?

DAVID RUNCORN

Simeon and Anna

Now there was a man in Jerusalem whose name was Simeon… [He was] looking forward to the consolation of Israel, and the Holy Spirit rested on him. It had been revealed to him by the Holy Spirit that he would not see death before he had seen the Lord's Messiah… There was also a prophet, Anna… She was of a great age, having lived with her husband for seven years after her marriage, then as a widow to the age of eighty-four… At that moment she came, and began to praise God and to speak about the child to all who were looking for the redemption of Jerusalem.

Simeon and Anna are well into their later years of life when the baby Jesus is brought to the temple. We know little else about them, but their faith and vision are clear to all. There are qualities here we may seek in the later years of our own lives.

They have grown old without losing hope. The turbulence, uncertainty and youthful indifference of this fast-changing world takes its toll over time. But their faith is still passionately alive.

They have known sorrow without growing bitter. After a brief marriage, Anna has lived as a vulnerable widow to over 80 years of age, but she is alive with positive purpose.

They have waited long without losing heart. There is no easy way to live patiently for things. Doubts can creep in over time. I particularly value and respect those who seem able to keep steady in hope when there is little on the surface to encourage them.

They have faced physical diminishment without losing personal value. In Rembrandt's painting of this scene, Simeon seems blind and immensely frail, but his face is shining as he holds the baby Jesus. Both he and Anna have a sense of steady confidence and worth about who they are before God. They have trusted what was promised.

Simeon and Anna encourage us to keep faith and vigil when what we hope for seems such a long time coming. And their eyes see what they have trusted unseen for so long.

Thank you for those I know who sustain faith and hope over time,
and help me to do the same. Amen

DAVID RUNCORN

On not knowing

Send out your bread upon the waters, for after many days you will get it back... Just as you do not know how the breath comes to the bones in the mother's womb, so you do not know the work of God, who makes everything. In the morning sow your seed, and at evening do not let your hands be idle; for you do not know which will prosper, this or that, or whether both alike will be good.

One of the tougher realities of life is accepting that whatever enterprise we undertake, we never have enough information to guarantee success. Nothing is risk free. After doing all we can to choose wisely and responsibly, things may simply not turn out how we hoped or expected. In our years of life, we can find ourselves looking back on a mixed story of plans laid and frustrated outcomes. Perhaps you have particular examples of that. But life is given to us to live. After saying our prayers, listening to the wisdom of friends and pondering the options before us, it is for us to act, to take risks and to make choices – great and small.

What we do not know is a repeated theme in Ecclesiastes. This does not leave the writer cynical or mistrusting. 'Sow your seeds,' says the teacher. But we must let go of our need to be in control. It is simply not possible. In later years, when we can feel acutely our growing inability to manage outcomes our own way, there is challenging wisdom in this.

Christian faith is not the promise of guaranteed outcomes. The best-prayed-for things can and do go painfully wrong. But the promise is that the deepest source of life is always God, 'who makes everything' and is ever-present in it all. The apostle Paul expresses the tension this way: 'Work out your own salvation with fear and trembling,' he writes, before going on to point out that something deeper is going on – 'for it is God who is at work in you... to work for his good pleasure' (Philippians 2:12–13). God delights to journey with us, whatever the outcomes.

'God, grant me the serenity to accept the things I cannot change, courage to change the things I can and wisdom to know the difference'
(Reinhold Niebuhr, 1892–1971).

DAVID RUNCORN

The rejoicing habit

Rejoice in the Lord always; again I will say, Rejoice. Let your gentleness be known to everyone. The Lord is near. Do not worry about anything, but in everything by prayer and supplication with thanksgiving let your requests be made known to God. And the peace of God, which surpasses all understanding, will guard your hearts and your minds in Christ Jesus. Finally, beloved, whatever is true, whatever is honourable, whatever is just, whatever is pure, whatever is pleasing, whatever is commendable, if there is any excellence and if there is anything worthy of praise, think about these things.

The letter to the Philippians was written to a vulnerable church by a man who was in prison for his faith. So we might not expect rejoicing to be a main theme in the letter. But 'joy', 'rejoicing' and 'thanksgiving' are words repeated throughout.

This is something more profound than wishful optimism or an avoidance of the tough realities of life. It is a theological conviction based upon the character and faithfulness of God. Pope Francis' first papal letter was about joy. 'Our Christian joy drinks from Jesus' brimming heart,' he wrote. This sets all our responses to life in the context of trusting faith. It helps build our faith in what God is doing and refuses to allow the bad news to be the final story.

This needs to become a habit. Our physical muscles need regular exercise if we are to stay fit and agile. The same is true of our emotional and spiritual responses to life. Rejoicing, for Paul, needs to be practised until it becomes a faithful reflex for a lifetime. We must use it or lose it.

Rejoicing resists world-weariness and cynicism. It is the antidote to demoralisation and hopelessness in a world seemingly full of bad news. It subverts the prevailing scripts. It insists there is another story being told. For the Lord is near. It always sounds like a contradiction. The Romanian pastor Richard Wurmbrand wrote of how he learned to rejoice in the Lord in prison despite torture and dreadful conditions.

Practise a response of joy today in the midst of your life,
in all its circumstances. The Lord is near.

DAVID RUNCORN

Hidden with Christ

If you have been raised with Christ, seek the things that are above, where Christ is, seated at the right hand of God. Set your minds on things that are above, not on things that are on earth, for you have died, and your life is hidden with Christ in God. When Christ who is your life is revealed, then you also will be revealed with him in glory.

These verses challenge us as to what we make the focus of our lives. Keep your hope and vision fixed on Christ, says Paul. But there are times when circumstances can leave us without the resources for sustaining faith and discipleship in that way – when we are living with serious illness, perhaps, or with the mental and physical incapacity that can come with ageing. There are times when it is just not possible to pray or make such conscious acts of faith. We do not have the energy. We cannot even think straight. What are we to do then? I remember sitting by the bedside of someone in intensive care. Every remaining ounce of their energy was needed to draw their next breath.

There is a verse in this passage that offers a particular encouragement for such times. 'Your life is hidden with Christ,' says Paul. When I say, 'My faith is in Christ,' I am expressing my conscious choice and commitment to be a follower of Jesus and to trust him for my life and salvation. But I am saying much more than that. I have given my life to Christ. He holds it in love. It is secure with him. To say 'My faith is in Christ' means much more than my own act of will or understanding. I am declaring where it is to be found – held safe and secure. Christ holds my faith.

A woman living with cancer tells of how this verse sustained and even freed her. She realised she did not have to sustain the effort of keeping her faith in Christ. She had given it all to him and was safe, hidden in his love. All shall be well.

Lord Jesus, thank you for holding and keeping safe
what I cannot sustain by my own strength. Amen

DAVID RUNCORN

The final journey

The last enemy to be destroyed is death… What is sown is perishable, what is raised is imperishable. It is sown in dishonour, it is raised in glory. It is sown in weakness, it is raised in power. It is sown a physical body, it is raised a spiritual body. If there is a physical body, there is also a spiritual body… When this perishable body puts on imperishability, and this mortal body puts on immortality, then the saying that is written will be fulfilled: 'Death has been swallowed up in victory.' 'Where, O death, is your victory? Where, O death, is your sting?'

Death brings our human journey to completion. When the ancient litany asks God to save us from, among other things, 'sudden death', we are praying for time to be rightly prepared for a day and time we cannot predict. We are to be as ready as we can be.

This is a bittersweet reality for even the strongest of faith. From our earthly perspective, death remains 'the last enemy'. There is grief and loss to endure. But it is also the place where Christ is revealed in resurrection life. He will meet us there and our journey of faith unseen will come at last to joyful sight.

For many years, my friend John lived with a chronic heart condition. He was very close to death numerous times. His moving testimony offers a glimpse into the mystery of this place: 'Death is very natural when you get there… so welcoming and warm, assuring of well-being. It means home and it feels like home when you get there. I, for a little while, stood in the doorway and I know what it is like.'

In the hymn to creation, 'Canticle of the Sun', attributed to Francis of Assisi, death is called to praise God with these words: 'O thou most kind and gentle death, waiting to hush our latest breath. O praise him, Alleluia! Thou leadest home the child of God, and Christ our Lord the way has trod. O praise him, Alleluia!' It is a long hymn and this verse is nearly always omitted. But it needs including. It is part of the song of life and the threshold to the full presence of Christ.

Sing or read the verse of that hymn once more.

DAVID RUNCORN

Psalm 43—56:
songs of a threatened people

 For many years I've waited for someone to write a book on the Bible and international relations. If I were a book editor I would certainly commission one! After all, most of the Bible is the story of a small, vulnerable nation surrounded by changing superpowers, trying to negotiate the shifting power relations that affected it in its struggle to survive. Admittedly, it had God on its side, but that did not automatically protect it from invasion, economic collapse or natural disaster. The prophets always made it clear that possession of the land was dependent on obeying God's commands to do justice and promote the well-being of all the land's people, including its immigrants.

Some of the psalms we will look at over the next fortnight arise from specific situations in the life of David, their main writer. But mostly they are set on a wider canvas of the nation of Israel/Judah and the threats it faces. So we can validly use them to address national and global situations in our own time, though always remembering that no nation today is specifically chosen by God, as the 'children of Israel' were then. God's people today are a worldwide entity, focused on, but not necessarily limited to, what we define as the church.

As we read these varied songs of worship, we need to remember that they were used in the regular liturgy of the Jewish people and to think about whether the range of emotions and situations we bring into our own worship reflects the range covered in these psalms. Do the worship songs and hymns we sing address the challenges and opportunities we face Monday to Saturday, and not just our desire to praise God on a Sunday? If you are a worship leader, how might you use these psalms in your worship to bring our own social and political situations into our communal time with God? In particular, we might ask how our worship addresses the fears and hopes of those who live a less privileged life, in countries with less stable government and less adequate public services. We might also ask how we can use the inspiration of these psalms to challenge bad governance and to call for and create a fairer and more just society.

VERONICA ZUNDEL

113

Alone against the world?

Vindicate me, O God, and defend my cause against an ungodly people; from those who are deceitful and unjust deliver me! For you are the God in whom I take refuge; why have you cast me off? Why must I walk about mournfully because of the oppression of the enemy? O send out your light and your truth; let them lead me; let them bring me to your holy hill and to your dwelling. Then I will go to the altar of God, to God my exceeding joy; and I will praise you with the harp, O God, my God.

How are we to act as Christians when we have no faith in those who govern us? Millions of people around the world live under unjust or deceitful rule. Even in the 'democratic' west we are not immune. And even if we do have a government we trust, we can still find the culture around us greedy, violent or just plain selfish.

Psalm 43 is essentially a continuation of Psalm 42, and they have often been treated as a single psalm, dealing with what some call 'spiritual depression'. However, this section does introduce a new idea – that the psalmist is battling not just against individual enemies but against a whole people. Not only that, but he is also the one being treated as in the wrong.

In these circumstances we may have no recourse but to cry out to God to protect us. In times of darkness, we need the light and truth of God's Spirit to bring us back to a place where we can again worship and feel the joy of God's presence. The implication here is that this is a communal place, where God's people can rediscover a community of hope, supporting each other in a hostile environment – and can go on to act.

As I write, the coronavirus pandemic is leading some churches to offer online worship or to livestream their services for those who are self-isolating. My hope is that when you read this, Christians will again be able to gather freely. In the meantime, we have had to find creative ways of encouraging each other. Let us hope the best ones have survived!

---

*Pray for those who live in an environment where Christians
and those who act for justice are actively persecuted.*

VERONICA ZUNDEL

When the boat rocks

We have heard with our ears, O God, our ancestors have told us, what deeds you performed in their days, in the days of old: you with your own hand drove out the nations, but them you planted; you afflicted the peoples, but them you set free… Yet you have rejected us and abased us, and have not gone out with our armies. You made us turn back from the foe, and our enemies have taken spoil for themselves. You have made us like sheep for slaughter, and have scattered us among the nations… Rouse yourself! Why do you sleep, O Lord? Awake, do not cast us off forever! Why do you hide your face?… Rise up, come to our help. Redeem us for the sake of your steadfast love.

Many outreach efforts by churches seem to want to take us back to a time when we were a 'Christian nation'. Ecclesiastes has no time for such an approach: 'Do not say, "Why were the former days better than these?" For it is not from wisdom that you ask this' (Ecclesiastes 7:10). It is understandable that the psalmist wants to hark back to the times he has heard about, when God's people prospered and experienced miraculous provision. But God is always in the business of doing 'a new thing' (Isaiah 43:19), and we are to look forward, not back. This is a challenge to those of us who have more past than future on this earth, but we should never give up being ready for change.

When life is hard for us, individually or as a community, it is tempting to think God has stopped caring. Jesus' disciples felt this fear when he literally fell asleep in a boat with them on a rough lake stirred up by a storm. I find it comforting that both they and the psalmist here had no qualms about saying, 'Wake up, Lord!' If we're feeling as if we're sheep headed for the abattoir, God has no problem with our saying so. But notice that here the writer also reminds God (and himself?) that God has a history of 'steadfast love'. Even if we forget God, God does not forget us.

'Teacher, do you not care that we are perishing?' (Mark 4:38).

VERONICA ZUNDEL

Power and duty

My heart overflows with a goodly theme; I address my verses to the king; my tongue is like the pen of a ready scribe. You are the most handsome of men; grace is poured upon your lips; therefore God has blessed you forever. Gird your sword on your thigh, O mighty one, in your glory and majesty. In your majesty ride on victoriously for the cause of truth and to defend the right; let your right hand teach you dread deeds... Hear, O daughter, consider and incline your ear; forget your people and your father's house, and the king will desire your beauty... In the place of ancestors you, O king, shall have sons; you will make them princes in all the earth. I will cause your name to be celebrated in all generations; therefore the peoples will praise you forever and ever.

We are all ready to criticise bad government, but do we ever praise good government? The writer here is acting as a kind of poet laureate, composing a song complimenting the king, possibly on the occasion of his marriage.

We might see this as toadying to the powers that be, but there is genuine challenge here, too. To praise the king for his handsomeness might be flattery, but to exhort him to 'ride on victoriously for the cause of truth and to defend the right' is a call to rule in the name of God, to do justice and love mercy and not just to attain military victories. The ancient Jews had absolute monarchy, while we have democracy, but the duty to govern for the benefit of all is the same (see King Lemuel's advice from his mother in Proverbs 31:8–9).

In the middle of this psalm, the writer turns to praising God as king, and then back to the earthly king. This gives the psalm a messianic slant, suggesting not only that the king is God's representative, but that only God can fully embody this perfect kingship. But remember that when Jesus came, his kingship was so different to the rule the people expected that most did not recognise him as a king at all.

'You love righteousness and hate wickedness' (v. 7). Is there a politician past or present of whom you could say that? Pray for them.

VERONICA ZUNDEL

Stop fighting; stop fearing

God is our refuge and strength, a very present help in trouble. Therefore we will not fear, though the earth should change, though the mountains shake in the heart of the sea; though its waters roar and foam, though the mountains tremble with its tumult… Come, behold the works of the Lord; see what desolations he has brought on the earth. He makes wars cease to the end of the earth; he breaks the bow, and shatters the spear; he burns the shields with fire. 'Be still, and know that I am God! I am exalted among the nations, I am exalted in the earth.' The Lord of hosts is with us; the God of Jacob is our refuge.

How would you feel if asked to contemplate 'what desolations God has brought on the earth'? It doesn't sound very encouraging, does it? But when you read the context, you can see that the desolation refers to the complete destruction of the arms industry and the whole machinery of war. That's the sort of desolation that would benefit us all!

That's why I prefer an alternative translation of that famous verse that begins 'Be still', which forms the opening of a Mennonite worship song: 'Stop fighting, and know that I am God.' The call to 'be still' may be very good for our spiritual health, but the call to 'stop fighting' would be good for our whole world. We have the capacity now, in our stockpile of nuclear armaments, to destroy the world several times over; even the UK's 'small' nuclear armoury is enough for thousands of Hiroshimas. Instead of the threat of such devastation, wouldn't we prefer to see God's destruction of our foolish addiction to violence and the threat of violence?

But, of course, the task is not all God's. We who follow the prince of peace are to act on his agenda to bring peace to the nations. That action should not be out of fear – this psalm tells us not to be afraid even in the most frightening circumstances – but out of love for the world God created and is working to renew.

What frightens you most at the moment? Take that fear to God,
then ask what action you can take to change it.

VERONICA ZUNDEL

Extending the borders

Clap your hands, all you peoples; shout to God with loud songs of joy. For the Lord, the Most High, is awesome, a great king over all the earth. He subdued peoples under us, and nations under our feet. He chose our heritage for us, the pride of Jacob whom he loves. God has gone up with a shout, the Lord with the sound of a trumpet. Sing praises to God, sing praises; sing praises to our King, sing praises. For God is the king of all the earth; sing praises with a psalm.

You can learn a lot by pursuing the word 'all' through the Bible. Verses that immediately come to mind are: 'Through him God was pleased to reconcile to himself all things, whether on earth or in heaven' (Colossians 1:20) and 'The Lord is not slow about his promise, as some think of slowness, but is patient with you, not wanting any to perish, but all to come to repentance' (2 Peter 3:9).

So far our psalms have focused on the situation of God's chosen people. And here, too, 'the pride of Jacob' is marked out as a special locus of God's love. This psalm, however, goes much further. It may be the task of the chosen people to point the way to the one God and to initiate God's praise, but the rest of the world is expected to join in. Because the God of Israel is also the God of the whole world, the inheritance of Israel is to be extended to all peoples.

Despite numerous messages from the Old Testament prophets reminding the Israelites that their mission was to be 'a light to the nations', the first Christians were very slow to catch on to the idea that their new faith in Jesus was for all, regardless of their origin. The big debate in the early church was whether non-Jews were allowed to join (ironic when we consider how small a minority those of Jewish descent are in today's churches). If the Jesus movement had remained a Jewish sect, the world would look very different today. God's plans are always bigger than we think.

Is there a group of people you regard as outside God's mercy?
Pray for them.

VERONICA ZUNDEL

God's new address

Great is the Lord and greatly to be praised in the city of our God. His holy mountain, beautiful in elevation is the joy of all the earth… Then the kings assembled, they came on together. As soon as they saw it, they were astounded; they were in panic, they took to flight; trembling took hold of them there, pains as of a woman in labour, as when an east wind shatters the ships of Tarshish… Walk about Zion, go all around it, count its towers, consider well its ramparts; go through its citadels, that you may tell the next generation that this is God, our God forever and ever. He will be our guide forever.

Over 40 years ago, I remember arriving in Jerusalem from Galilee on a bus, having caught a bug, been sick and delirious all night and still feeling extremely ill. As the coach circled the walls before it entered the old city, I thought to myself, 'I have seen the walls of Jerusalem, I can die now!'

Most of us have special places, spots where we have had an unexpected encounter with God or where we feel we habitually meet with God, whether that's a retreat house, the church where we meet weekly or even a car park at midnight (where one high-profile Christian claims she had her converting experience of God).

For the ancient Israelites, Jerusalem, the site of their temple, was especially revered: it was where they offered their worship to God, where they went on pilgrimage every year and, most of all, the visible sign on earth of their God's presence with them. As well as a source of joy to God's people, it was seen as a source of fear to those who did not honour God.

All the more shocking, then, when Jesus predicts to his followers that 'not one stone will be left here upon another' (Matthew 24:2). He is ushering in a new era when the temple of God will be built not of dressed stones, but of 'living stones' (1 Peter 2:5): a temple built of people, of you and me.

What would it mean to 'walk about Zion', 'consider well its ramparts' and 'go through its citadels' in relation to this new, human temple?

VERONICA ZUNDEL

Ransomed

Why should I fear in times of trouble, when the iniquity of my persecutors surrounds me, those who trust in their wealth and boast of the abundance of their riches? Truly, no ransom avails for one's life, there is no price one can give to God for it. For the ransom of life is costly, and can never suffice, that one should live on forever and never see the grave… Such is the fate of the foolhardy, the end of those who are pleased with their lot. Like sheep they are appointed for Sheol; Death shall be their shepherd; straight to the grave they descend, and their form shall waste away; Sheol shall be their home. But God will ransom my soul from the power of Sheol, for he will receive me.

A political leader was recently reported as saying, 'People are dying who have never died before'! I think I know what he really meant: that new categories of people were dying unexpectedly, people who might have enjoyed many more years of life. And that is, of course, tragic. But none of us can avoid death: we are all held hostage to our own mortality, and no earthly ransom is high enough to redeem us from it.

Yet even amid this gloomy outlook, the psalmist finds room for hope. Old Testament understanding of an afterlife was patchy and vague; the dead went to Sheol, a shadowy realm of oblivion. Nevertheless, the psalmist's faith in God, and God's love for him, are such that he can picture a time when God will renew his life and rescue him from the grave. It is a tantalising glimpse of a love that is stronger than death.

We know that the unpayable ransom has been paid by God in Christ, a death to overcome death. Because of this, we are not to be envious of the powerful in this life, for they have no such hope; in Jesus' memorable phrase, they 'store up treasures for themselves but are not rich towards God' (Luke 12:21).

'I know that my Redeemer lives, and that at the last he will stand upon the earth; and after my skin has been thus destroyed, then in my flesh I shall see God' (Job 19:25–26).

VERONICA ZUNDEL

Hungry for justice

'Hear, O my people, and I will speak, O Israel, I will testify against you. I am God, your God. Not for your sacrifices do I rebuke you; your burnt-offerings are continually before me. I will not accept a bull from your house, or goats from your folds. For every wild animal of the forest is mine, the cattle on a thousand hills. I know all the birds of the air, and all that moves in the field is mine. If I were hungry, I would not tell you, for the world and all that is in it is mine. Do I eat the flesh of bulls, or drink the blood of goats? Offer to God a sacrifice of thanksgiving, and pay your vows to the Most High. Call on me in the day of trouble; I will deliver you, and you shall glorify me.'

At 14 I became a vegetarian. Life had become more difficult and I felt the need to make some sort of sacrifice. Being only 14, there were not many vices I had yet taken up, so meat was the only thing I could give up.

Most of us have the impulse to make sacrifices in the hope that they will improve our lives. The religious life of the Jewish people at the time the psalms were written revolved around sacrifices of animals and agricultural produce. These, they believed, would cancel out their sins and put them back in God's favour. After all, such actions were prescribed in the law of Moses, the first five books of the Bible.

In this context, I am struck by how radical this psalm is. It is written to be sung in the temple, the place where all those sacrifices are made, yet its whole message undermines those very attempts to appease God. Would we sing something on a Sunday that declared how meaningless our worship is without obedience?

God is not in need of our offerings. Instead, the psalmist says, 'to those who go the right way I will show the salvation of God' (v. 23). Right behaviour is worth more than impeccable worship; wrong behaviour cancels out any attempts to get God on our side.

'Go and learn what this means, "I desire mercy, not sacrifice"'
(Matthew 9:13; see Hosea 6:6).

VERONICA ZUNDEL

The heart of the matter

Have mercy on me, O God, according to your steadfast love; according to your abundant mercy blot out my transgressions… For I know my transgressions, and my sin is ever before me… Create in me a clean heart, O God, and put a new and right spirit within me. Do not cast me away from your presence, and do not take your holy spirit from me. Restore to me the joy of your salvation, and sustain in me a willing spirit. Then I will teach transgressors your ways, and sinners will return to you.

'Power tends to corrupt, and absolute power corrupts absolutely,' said the Victorian politician Lord Acton. David, once he becomes king, demonstrates this dramatically. His abduction and rape of Bathsheba (there is no suggestion that she has a choice) and his engineering of her husband's death are the behaviour of a tyrant (see 2 Samuel 11).

David's sins are of the body (his predatory behaviour) and of the mind (his plot to murder Uriah). Yet it is his heart – considered by ancient Jews to be the seat of the will – that he wants cleansed. He knows that evil arises in our inner attitudes: women are commodities; soldiers, even the most faithful, are disposable. As Jeremiah tells us, 'The heart is devious above all else; it is perverse – who can understand it?' (Jeremiah 17:9).

Yet it is Jeremiah, too, who promises the change David longs for: 'But this is the covenant that I will make with the house of Israel after those days, says the Lord: I will put my law within them, and I will write it on their hearts' (Jeremiah 31:33). To have God's law written on our hearts is to do the right thing instinctively – what one of the founders of my Mennonite congregation called being 're-reflexed'. This is a long process, and we are all still a long way from its completion. But if we have given our lives to Jesus, we are gradually learning to walk in his Spirit.

'If we walk in the light as he himself is in the light, we have fellowship with one another, and the blood of Jesus his Son cleanses us from all sin'
(1 John 1:7).

VERONICA ZUNDEL

Naming evil

Why do you boast, O mighty one, of mischief done against the godly? All day long you are plotting destruction. Your tongue is like a sharp razor, you worker of treachery. You love evil more than good, and lying more than speaking the truth. You love all words that devour, O deceitful tongue. But God will break you down forever; he will snatch and tear you from your tent; he will uproot you from the land of the living… But I am like a green olive tree in the house of God. I trust in the steadfast love of God forever and ever. I will thank you forever, because of what you have done. In the presence of the faithful I will proclaim your name, for it is good.

The Quakers have a practice that they call 'speaking truth to power'. It's what Nathan did to David when he challenged him on his behaviour in regard to Bathsheba. It's a dangerous undertaking, which can get you killed. Nathan was clever about it: he told David a parable, which got David enraged about the actions of the villain of the parable – until David realised with a little prompting that he himself was the villain (see 2 Samuel 12). Likewise Jesus himself challenged the political leaders of his day (he called Herod 'that fox').

Is there a danger here of being judgemental or hypocritical, of pointing out the speck in our neighbour's eye and ignoring the plank in our own? We certainly need to be sure of our own integrity before questioning that of others, but we do not have to be perfect before we can point out 'wickedness in high places' (Ephesians 6:12, KJV). Jesus' early followers stood up fearlessly to the authorities who sought to silence them.

All this calls for both wisdom and courage. Today's psalm is another linked to a particular incident in David's life, when an enemy betrayed his whereabouts to Saul, who was trying to kill him. He had no hesitation in expressing his opinion of such an action, because he was confident of his own calling from God, to reign in place of the increasingly compromised Saul.

'The word that you hear is not mine, but is from the Father who sent me'
(John 14:24). May our words, too, be from God.

VERONICA ZUNDEL

Original sin or original blessing?

Fools say in their hearts, 'There is no God.' They are corrupt, they commit abominable acts; there is no one who does good. God looks down from heaven on humankind to see if there are any who are wise, who seek after God. They have all fallen away, they are all alike perverse; there is no one who does good, no, not one… O that deliverance for Israel would come from Zion! When God restores the fortunes of his people, Jacob will rejoice; Israel will be glad.

I write at the height of the Covid-19 pandemic, which has brought out both the worst and the best in people. Some are scamming the vulnerable, taking money to do their shopping and then not returning or selling fake tests or treatments. Others are looking out for their neighbours, offering help and starting new community groups. Churches are streaming online worship in place of face-to-face gatherings, and a side effect of this is that those who have been housebound for years are being included for the first time.

So, is humankind basically good or basically bad? Perhaps our take on this varies according to what mood we are in or to the circumstances around us. The psalmist is certainly in an 'everyone is horrible' mood! The world seems full of contempt, corruption and cynicism. As 'in the days of Noah' (1 Peter 3:20), God contemplates humanity and is hard-pressed to find any who believe in anything more than their own advantage.

And yet, even in the Noah story, God finds a family of eight who still honour God and seek to do what is right. Even in the story of Sodom, where Abraham bargains with God as to how many righteous in the city would persuade God to hold back on its destruction (Genesis 18:23–33), God rescues Lot and his family from the cataclysm.

Julian of Norwich's visions taught her that 'in every soul that is to be saved, there is a godly will that has never consented to sin'. I think she means that we all still bear the image of God, given in our creation, however obscured it may be. Salvation is the process of restoring it.

Think of the person you find hardest to like.
What can you find that is good in them?

VERONICA ZUNDEL

Future present

Save me, O God, by your name, and vindicate me by your might. Hear my prayer, O God; give ear to the words of my mouth. For the insolent have risen against me, the ruthless seek my life; they do not set God before them. But surely, God is my helper; the Lord is the upholder of my life. He will repay my enemies for their evil. In your faithfulness, put an end to them. With a freewill-offering I will sacrifice to you; I will give thanks to your name, O Lord, for it is good. For he has delivered me from every trouble, and my eye has looked in triumph on my enemies.

Bible scholars have a concept called 'realised eschatology' (eschatology being the study of the end times), which is when a prophet talks of the future renewal of creation as if it has already happened. Their faith in God's purposes is enough to make them certain that those purposes will be realised.

David is doing something similar here, but on a smaller and more immediate scale. This is another psalm linked by its heading to a time before his kingship, when he is running from an angry King Saul and when those who were supposed to be protecting him have betrayed him. Perhaps because he is in a hurry to escape, this psalm is short enough for us to reproduce it in full here. He begins by pleading to God for rescue, but by the end he is praising God for delivering him, even though he is actually still at great risk.

Such faith can only be based on past experience: because God has delivered David from every danger so far, he is confident that God will do it again. In the first and penultimate verses he invokes God's name, 'for it is good'. In other words, in his eyes God has a reputation for saving people. Today we might say that God's reviews are positive!

Think back to times in the past when God has rescued you from external or internal dangers, and thank God for those times.

VERONICA ZUNDEL

Faithlessness in the city

My heart is in anguish within me, the terrors of death have fallen upon me. Fear and trembling come upon me, and horror overwhelms me. And I say, 'O that I had wings like a dove! I would fly away and be at rest; truly, I would flee far away; I would lodge in the wilderness'... Confuse, O Lord, confound their speech; for I see violence and strife in the city. Day and night they go around it on its walls, and iniquity and trouble are within it; ruin is in its midst; oppression and fraud do not depart from its market-place. It is not enemies who taunt me – I could bear that... But it is you, my equal, my companion, my familiar friend, with whom I kept pleasant company; we walked in the house of God with the throng... But you, O God, will cast them down into the lowest pit; the bloodthirsty and treacherous shall not live out half their days. But I will trust in you.

In the midst of a global crisis, this psalm speaks profoundly to our fears and griefs. I hope that by the time you read this, the Covid-19 crisis will be over, but there will be many across the world who are mourning key people in their life and who may be justifiably angry about their government's actions or inaction.

None of this is new. Since the earliest days of humanity, as the Eden story tells us, there have been betrayal and suspicion, blame and aggression, natural disasters and personal losses. How we would all like to escape this turmoil. Right now, I would love to go on a retreat, but they have all been cancelled because of the crisis.

David here laments the treachery of a close friend. But we should remember that David himself betrayed his loyal servant Uriah when he wanted to grab Uriah's wife. In a world where corruption and violence destroy our 'safe spaces' (the city was meant to be a haven from the dangers of the wilderness), we cannot pretend we are entirely innocent. We are all caught up in 'the system' and benefit from its iniquities.

'Guard me as the apple of the eye; hide me in the shadow of your wings'
(Psalm 17:8)

VERONICA ZUNDEL

Be not afraid

Be gracious to me, O God, for people trample on me; all day long foes oppress me; my enemies trample on me all day long, for many fight against me. O Most High, when I am afraid, I put my trust in you. In God, whose word I praise, in God I trust; I am not afraid; what can flesh do to me?… You have kept count of my tossings; put my tears in your bottle. Are they not in your record? Then my enemies will retreat on the day when I call. This I know, that God is for me. In God, whose word I praise, in the Lord, whose word I praise, in God I trust; I am not afraid.

Just after my church closed down, we held a day together, inviting many past members and sharing reminiscences of its 40-year life. One of the songs we sang was the beautiful 'Be not afraid' by Bob Dufford and John Michael Talbot. I've been thinking of that song often recently, in a time of worldwide fear.

In moments of panic, we can believe that no one knows how we are feeling, that we have been forgotten and no one will notice when we are gone. This psalm's wonderful image of God saving up our tears in a bottle is an antidote to that feeling. It reminds me of the woman who appears in all the gospels, washing Jesus' feet with her tears and pouring a vial of priceless perfume over them (see, for instance, Luke 7:36–50). Our tears, shed or unshed, are precious to God; they are an offering poured at God's feet, an offering which is noticed and recorded.

It is hard for many of us, especially those who suffer from mental illness, to declare, 'In God I trust; I am not afraid.' Our fears run deep and may have plagued us for years. God does not condemn us for fearfulness; even Jesus was afraid, in Gethsemane, the night before his crucifixion. But like David, we can choose to act as though we were not afraid, and sometimes, miraculously, we will find that, in so acting, we are indeed not afraid any more.

'Peace I leave with you; my peace I give to you' (John 14:27).

VERONICA ZUNDEL

Acts 12—15

Those of you with good memories will recall that, a little over a year ago, there was a series of reflections on Acts 9—11. Over the next ten days we are going to look at a few more chapters, and what an action-packed section of the book it is!

First, it includes and involves some interesting characters: Peter, Paul and Barnabas obviously, but also John Mark, who was to write the first gospel. James the brother of Jesus comes to the fore, too, for he became the leader of the church in Jerusalem.

Second, these chapters feature some key moments and shifts in the development of the early church. The first of these transitions revolves around some of the players noted above, for it is during these chapters that we see the spotlight shifting from Peter to Paul; indeed, after chapter 15 we do not meet Peter again in Acts. In a similar vein, in terms of the missionary journeys, we see leadership transferred from Barnabas to Paul in Acts 13:13.

A related and very significant shift is that of focusing more and more upon presenting the gospel message to the Gentiles – in fact, chapter 15 is devoted almost entirely to a meeting of church leaders in Jerusalem when the justification for that shift was thrashed out.

Next, how many of you remember those school lessons on Paul's missionary journeys? We have the first journey in full here and the introduction to the second.

Finally and more generally, one could be forgiven for thinking that Luke is doing no more than telling a story in Acts; it reads as straightforward narrative. But it is much subtler than that; there are all sorts of patterns within the book, and in many ways it is a mirror of Luke's gospel.

This book is sometimes called the gospel of the Holy Spirit, for it tells the story of God's Spirit being active in the lives of the early Christians as he was active in the life of Jesus.

GEOFF LOWSON

The potential of power

About that time King Herod laid violent hands upon some who belonged to the church. He had James, the brother of John, killed with the sword. After he saw that it pleased the Jews, he proceeded to arrest Peter also. (This was during the festival of Unleavened Bread.) When he had seized him, he put him in prison and handed him over to four squads of soldiers to guard him, intending to bring him out to the people after the Passover.

The King Herod in this passage (there were six Herods) was Herod Agrippa I, grandson of Herod the Great, whom we remember so vividly from the story of the three wise men. Agrippa was brought up in Rome, where he made many influential friends, including Claudius and Caligula; the latter bestowed Palestinian territory upon him. But despite being close to the Romans, Herod, being very shrewd, courted the Jewish authorities too, being careful to respect the law and Jewish traditions. Consequently, he was popular with the people. This attack on the early church by killing James and attempting to kill Peter was a purely political move to find favour with the Jewish powerbrokers.

Power is interesting. It is rather like the wind – you can't see it, but you can see its results. The word 'power' has its roots in the Latin *potentia*. In power there is potential – but potential for what? Herod used his power for evil, and how many examples of that can we think of in our world today?

In his letter to the Ephesians, Paul famously talks of 'principalities and powers'. In the world of that time, evil was linked with supernatural powers, spiritual rulers and so on. But Paul moves towards defining evil much more in terms of humans being the source of evil, rather than evil being outside humankind. And of course, it can be argued that corporate power can give rise to corporate evil, one classic example of which was apartheid. The debate about evil goes on.

But very importantly, power, whether individual or corporate, can be used for good. As Christians, we should take our lead from Jesus, who constantly stressed the power of servanthood rather than oppression.

'The measure of a man is what he does with power' (Plato).

GEOFF LOWSON

A story within a story

He went to the house of Mary, the mother of John whose other name was Mark, where many had gathered and were praying. When he knocked at the outer gate, a maid named Rhoda came to answer. On recognising Peter's voice, she was so overjoyed that, instead of opening the gate, she ran in and announced that Peter was standing at the gate. They said to her, 'You are out of your mind!'… Meanwhile, Peter continued knocking; and when they opened the gate, they saw him and were amazed. He… described for them how the Lord had brought him out of the prison. And he added, 'Tell this to James and to the believers.'

In a regular segment of the comedy sketch show *The Two Ronnies*, Ronnie Corbett, in his signature chair, would begin a story, then get sidetracked, only to come back to the original story and finish it off. That literary trick is called 'intercalation' and we have an example here. Yesterday we heard about Herod, and we will finish that story tomorrow, but today, slotted in, we have the brief account of Peter's visit to the house of Mary, which introduces us, fleetingly, to the maid Rhoda.

Any commentary on Luke's writing will draw attention to the fact that he goes out of his way to include the part women played in the Christian story, and so what of Rhoda? She was probably about twelve years of age and, although a slave, it seems she was a Christian – why else would she have been so excited about Peter? In reading this story I am reminded of the painting by Holman Hunt called *The Light of the World*. It famously shows Jesus knocking on a door that has no handle and so can only be opened from the inside. So it was for Peter – to get into the house, the door had to be opened from the inside. Rhoda does not open the door, but what she does is encourage others to do so. She is already convinced, but the beauty of the story is that she paves the way for others to believe too.

Are there ways in which your faith can embolden others to 'open the door'?

GEOFF LOWSON

Yet the word continued

Now Herod was angry with the people of Tyre and Sidon. So they came to him in a body; and after winning over Blastus, the king's chamberlain, they asked for a reconciliation, because their country depended on the king's country for food. On an appointed day Herod put on his royal robes, took his seat on the platform and delivered a public address to them. The people kept shouting, 'The voice of a god, and not of a mortal!' And immediately, because he had not given the glory to God, an angel of the Lord struck him down, and he was eaten by worms and died. But the word of God continued to advance and gain adherents.

In the children's story *The Pine Tree* by Rose Dobbs, a little pine tree is dissatisfied with its plain looks and so wishes for leaves of gold. Sure enough, next morning the tree has gold leaves. The tree is so proud and self-satisfied. But disaster strikes – a woodcutter comes along and understandably strips off all the gold leaves, and the tree is left to its fate. With no leaves, it dies.

Like the pine tree, Herod's vanity was his downfall. More than that, however, he succumbed to the temptation of accepting the glory that belongs to God alone, and we see the consequences. Luke does not spare us the details.

Interestingly, this same story is also told by the Jewish historian Josephus, though he sets the story in the context of a festival to honour the Emperor Claudius. According to Josephus, Herod entered the theatre in Caesarea dressed in a robe of silver cloth; as the sun rose, the robe glinted in the brightness and the crowd shouted that a god had come among them. At this, Herod became very ill and he never recovered.

With that in mind, the last verse in our passage above is important; we could slip in the additional words '*despite all this* the word of God continued to advance'. There are five parallel passages in Acts; whenever the Jewish authorities, Herod or others tried to prevent the proclamation of the gospel, in the end God prevailed and the church grew.

---

*Pray for the church of our age, which suffers opposition
in many parts of the world.*

GEOFF LOWSON

131

Becoming a missionary church

Now in the church at Antioch there were prophets and teachers: Barnabas, Simeon who was called Niger, Lucius of Cyrene, Manaen a member of the court of Herod the ruler, and Saul. While they were worshipping the Lord and fasting, the Holy Spirit said, 'Set apart for me Barnabas and Saul for the work to which I have called them.' Then after fasting and praying they laid their hands on them and sent them off. So, being sent out by the Holy Spirit, they went down to Seleucia; and from there they sailed to Cyprus.

The last verses of chapter 12 and the beginning of chapter 13 mark a transition from an emphasis upon the Jewish Christians and the work and preaching of Peter, to an emphasis upon Paul and the reaching out to the Gentiles. Saul becomes Paul in Acts 13:9, and the change of name is no coincidence – Saul is a Jewish name; Paul is Greek.

It is easy and understandable to think of Acts as a straightforward narrative, for it gives a fairly chronological account of the development of the early church. But Luke's writing is more complex than we might think. In Acts we find distinct parallels between the first part of the book (Peter and friends) and the second (Paul and friends). It is not possible to list all of these, but here are just a few examples: both parts begin with a special manifestation of the Spirit: both have the healing of a lame man; Stephen is stoned and Paul is stoned; in both cases divine guidance leads the protagonists off in unplanned directions, which they then have to justify in Jerusalem; Peter and Paul are both jailed at a Jewish feast and both escape.

In the short passage above we read of the Holy Spirit taking the lead in 'setting apart' Paul and Barnabas for the next stage of God's mission. But importantly, that intervention by the Spirit is then affirmed by the church through fasting and prayer and the laying on of hands. It is the Spirit and the church working together.

'They laid their hands on them and sent them off' (v. 3).
Reflect on the fact that the church as a body had become missionary.
What about your church?

GEOFF LOWSON

Keep exploring

Paul and his companions set sail from Paphos and came to Perga in Pamphylia. John, however, left them and returned to Jerusalem; but they went on from Perga and came to Antioch in Pisidia. And on the sabbath day they went into the synagogue and sat down. After the reading of the law and the prophets, the officials of the synagogue sent them a message, saying, 'Brothers, if you have any word of exhortation for the people, give it.' So Paul stood up and with a gesture began to speak: 'You Israelites, and others who fear God, listen.'

It is an amusing truism that some newly ordained deacons try to cover the whole of Christian doctrine and theology in their first few sermons. I guess their enthusiasm is to be applauded! But in truth, Paul did almost the same when he preached to the people of Antioch.

The section which follows the passage above is important because it is the only complete sermon of Paul that we have, and so perhaps it gives us an idea of what he must have said more generally on his travels. The sermon must have been good, because at the end, Luke tells us, 'As Paul and Barnabas were going out, the people urged them to speak about these things again the next sabbath' (Acts 13:42).

Confession time: I am a believer in solid teaching sermons. I don't mean so-called 'Bible bashing', but teaching the faith and teaching it seriously and systematically – if for no other reason than that for many, the sermon is the only vehicle for that teaching. (I guess that this readership is an exception.) A basic understanding of biblical study, of elements of doctrine and of the nature of liturgy and worship all form a bedrock for our faith. But very importantly, exploring these issues gives rise to asking questions and developing the habit and skill of reflecting theologically. A sermon should answer some questions but also give rise to others.

Anyway, I would like to think that the real fan wants to know more!

'Proclaiming the whole will of God should be the goal – and the joy –
of every church and every preacher' (Billy Graham).

GEOFF LOWSON

Moving forward

When the Gentiles heard this, they were glad and praised the word of the Lord; and as many as had been destined for eternal life became believers. Thus the word of the Lord spread throughout the region. But the Jews incited the devout women of high standing and the leading men of the city, and stirred up persecution against Paul and Barnabas, and drove them out of their region. So they shook the dust off their feet in protest against them, and went to Iconium. And the disciples were filled with joy and with the Holy Spirit.

At a dear friend's funeral recently, his sons spoke movingly about their father teaching them not to dwell on being knocked back or knocked down, but rather to focus on moving on, looking for the positive and where and what to do next. Indeed, both boys, now in their late 30s, have had some ups and downs, but they have followed the advice they were given; they have 'shaken the dust off their feet' and moved forward.

That is exactly what the disciples did. Their visit to Antioch had been successful on the whole, but now they were being knocked back – indeed, more than that, they were being threatened. Both the establishment Jews and the 'women of high standing' reacted negatively because they had things to lose from this new way that was being taught – for the Jews, a loss of authority; for the women, a loss of security. And so, Paul and Barnabas moved on.

A particularly telling verse above is: 'Thus the word of the Lord spread' (v. 49). It seems the apostles had in fact done their job well and the Gentiles, having taken the gospel to heart, were propagating it themselves. That was the positive that came out of the time in Antioch – the embryonic church was beginning to take up the work itself. One of the great thrills of working for the mission agency USPG in the 1980s and 1990s was witnessing that transition whereby churches in the developing world became self-reliant.

Reflect on a time when you have had to shake the dust off your feet and on the positive that came out of it.

GEOFF LOWSON

Preparing for the future

They appointed elders for them in each congregation and with prayer and fasting committed them to the Lord in whom they had put their faith... When they had given the message at Perga, they went down to Attalia and from there set sail for Antioch, where they had originally been commended to the grace of God for the task which they had now completed. When they arrived and had called the congregation together, they reported all that God had done through them, and how he had thrown open the gates of faith to the Gentiles. And they stayed for some time with the disciples there.

In a small village church a short drive from where we live, there is a simple brass plaque which reads: 'In memory of Robert, first bishop of Cape Town, by whom this church was consecrated. 13 May 1853.'

Robert Gray (1809–70) was born in Sunderland and after ordination served in Wells and then two parishes in Durham Diocese. He became involved with SPG, and in 1847 was consecrated bishop of Cape Town. He arrived there the same year and then in 1848 he and his wife embarked upon what was to be a 3,000-mile missionary journey east to Grahamstown, then to the interior and back to Cape Town. In 1850, he covered 4,000 miles on another journey to Natal. His is a wonderful story, but the thing to note is that, as he journeyed, he established structures which later led to the establishment of the Church of the Province of Southern Africa (now the Anglican Church of Southern Africa).

Acts 13—14 tells of Paul's first journey through Asia Minor. It is estimated that he covered 1,500 miles on this journey and over 6,500 miles in total. Paul had been commissioned by God 'to bring my name before Gentiles and kings and before the people of Israel' (Act 9:15, NRSV). He did exactly that; in fact, if we want to be analytical about it, there is a pattern, for after he left Antioch he preached alternately to Jews then Gentiles three times before returning. More than that, however, he too set up structures so that the church could flourish on its own.

'God, bless Africa, guard her people, guide her leaders and give her peace, for Jesus Christ's sake. Amen' (Archbishop Trevor Huddleston).

GEOFF LOWSON

Trouble at t' mill

Now certain persons who had come down from Judea began to teach the brotherhood that those who were not circumcised in accordance with Mosaic practice could not be saved. That brought them into fierce dissension and controversy with Paul and Barnabas. And so it was arranged that these two and some others from Antioch should go up to Jerusalem to see the apostles and elders about this question.

About 25 years ago I attended a residential course at St Colm's College, Edinburgh. Much to the amusement of my fellow attendees, I became excited on finding that a previous occupant of my room, in 1910, had been Bishop Samuel Azariah of Dornakal in south India. Azariah was a major contributor to the World Missionary Conference held in Edinburgh that year. He was the first indigenous Indian bishop in the Anglican Communion – accolade enough – but he is remembered particularly because his address to the conference is regarded as marking the beginning of the ecumenical movement.

Back in India he began the work which, in 1945, found fulfilment in the formation of the Church of South India (CSI), uniting Anglicans, Congregationalists, Presbyterians and Methodists. The process was complex (it took 35 years), but the major sticking point was that some Anglicans felt that free church ministers should be reordained as Anglicans. They wanted others to become like them.

The 'fierce dissension and controversy' noted in today's passage revolved around a parallel issue: Jews wanted Gentiles to become like them. Certain Jews insisted that the message was only for the 'chosen people' and so for a Gentile to become part of the church, he must first accept Judaism, which, in turn, meant being circumcised and accepting Hebrew customs.

The situation in India was resolved after extensive dialogue and with mutually agreed conditions. As we will see tomorrow, the meeting in Jerusalem was likewise resolved by debate and compromise. Dr Dolittle asked the question, 'Why can't you, like me, like animals?', by which he was saying, 'Why can't you be more like me?' How often have we fallen into that trap?

'Holy God, fill us with the power of your Spirit that we may be your witnesses to the ends of the earth' (CSI).

GEOFF LOWSON

Powerful speeches

James summed up: 'My friends,' he said, 'listen to me. Simeon has told how it first happened that God took notice of the Gentiles, to choose from among them a people to bear his name; and this agrees with the words of the prophets, as Scripture has it: "Thereafter I will return and rebuild the fallen house of David; even from its ruins I will rebuild it, and set it up again, that they may seek the Lord: all the rest of mankind, and the Gentiles, whom I have claimed for my own. Thus says the Lord, whose work it is, made known long ago." My judgement therefore is that we should impose no irksome restrictions on those of the Gentiles who are turning to God.'

Yesterday we left Paul and Barnabas heading for Jerusalem to discuss the place of the Gentiles within the early church. This meeting, dated about AD50, is usually referred to as the Council of Jerusalem. Paul and Barnabas gave an account of their travels, Peter (Simeon) addressed the meeting and, in today's passage, we have James' contribution. They must have been powerful speeches, for after debate the council accepted James' guidance and sent a delegation to the Gentile Christians with a message of affirmation.

Powerful speeches can sometimes precipitate hinge moments. Martin Luther King's 'I have a dream', Emmeline Pankhurst's 'Freedom or death' and Winston Churchill's 'We shall fight on the beaches' are all examples of speeches that changed the course of history.

But let us be careful; Hitler was also a great orator, and he knew it. He wrote, 'Every great movement on this earth owes its growth to orators and not to great writers.' That is a sweeping statement, but it has some truth to it. There is a lesson for all of us and particularly those of us who, for whatever reason, sometimes have a platform from which to speak. We should use the privilege wisely and thoughtfully.

Finally, ponder for a moment the consequences had the decision gone the other way, and the Gentiles had been excluded. You probably would not be reading this!

'To be a light to lighten the Gentiles; and to be the glory of thy people Israel'
(Luke 2:32).

GEOFF LOWSON

137

A beckoning God

After some days Paul said to Barnabas, 'Come, let us return and visit the believers in every city where we proclaimed the word of the Lord and see how they are doing.' Barnabas wanted to take with them John called Mark. But Paul decided not to take with them one who had deserted them in Pamphylia and had not accompanied them in the work. The disagreement became so sharp that they parted company; Barnabas took Mark with him and sailed away to Cyprus. But Paul chose Silas and set out, the believers commending him to the grace of the Lord.

What a wonderful day to reflect upon Paul setting off on his second missionary journey, and indeed Barnabas on his – for today the church remembers the great northern missionary Aidan. Aidan was a monk on Iona, but in about AD635, at the invitation of King Oswald, he arrived in Northumbria and, from his base on the island of Lindisfarne, would journey throughout the kingdom proclaiming the gospel. Wonderfully, the king used to accompany him as his translator.

Aidan's life is described most beautifully by another northern saint, Bede, who writes of Aidan: 'Whatever people he met on his walks, whether high or low, he stopped and spoke to them. If they were heathen, he urged them to be baptised; and if they were already Christian, he strengthened their faith by word and deed.' This is what Paul did on his second journey; he went back to those in Galatia who were already Christian, but then he also 'spoke to the heathen', as Bede would put it.

On the lawn beside the ruins of Lindisfarne Priory there is a lovely statue of Aidan, symbolic torch in hand, standing looking out over the sea towards the mainland. My mind is taken forward to the next chapter of Paul's life; I have a mental image of Paul, who, after getting the call 'Come over to Macedonia and help us' (Acts 16:9), is looking out over the sea from Troas.

Beckoning God, as you called Aidan to Northumbria and as you called Paul to Macedonia and so Europe, open our ears and hearts as you beckon us.

GEOFF LOWSON

Become a Friend of BRF
and give regularly
to support our ministry

We help people of all ages to grow in faith

We encourage and support individual Christians and churches as they serve and resource the changing spiritual needs of communities today.

Through **Anna Chaplaincy** we're enabling churches to provide spiritual care to older people

Through **Living Faith** we're nurturing faith and resourcing life-long discipleship

Through **Messy Church** we're helping churches to reach out to families

Through **Parenting for Faith** we're supporting parents as they raise their children in the Christian faith

Our ministry is only possible because of the generous support of individuals, churches, trusts and gifts in wills.

As we look to the future and make plans, **regular donations make a huge difference** in ensuring we can both start and finish projects well.

By becoming a Friend of BRF and giving regularly to our ministry you are partnering with us in the gospel and helping change lives.

How your gift makes a difference

£2 a month — Helps us to develop **Living Faith** resources to use in care homes and communities

£10 a month — Helps us to support churches running the **Parenting for Faith** course and stand alongside parents

£5 a month — Helps us to support **Messy Church** volunteers and resource and grow the wider network

£20 a month — Helps us to resource **Anna Chaplaincy** and improve spiritual care for older people

 ## How to become a Friend of BRF

Set up a Direct Debit donation at **brf.org.uk/donate** or find out how to set up a Standing Order at **brf.org.uk/friends**

Contact the fundraising team

Email: **giving@brf.org.uk**
Tel: +44 (0)1235 462305
Post: Fundraising team, BRF, 15 The Chambers, Vineyard, Abingdon OX14 3FE

Good to know

If you have any questions, or if you want to change your regular donation or stop giving in the future, do get in touch.

Registered with

FR

FUNDRAISING
REGULATOR

I would like to make a donation to support BRF.
Please use my gift for:

☐ Where it is most needed ☐ Anna Chaplaincy ☐ Living Faith
☐ Messy Church ☐ Parenting for Faith

Title	First name/initials	Surname

Address	
	Postcode

Email

Telephone

Signature	Date

Our ministry is only possible because of the generous support of individuals, churches, trusts and gifts in wills.

giftaid it   You can add an extra 25p to every £1 you give.

Please treat as Gift Aid donations all qualifying gifts of money made

☐ today,   ☐ in the past four years,   ☐ and in the future.

I am a UK taxpayer and understand that if I pay less Income Tax and/or Capital Gains Tax in the current tax year than the amount of Gift Aid claimed on all my donations, it is my responsibility to pay any difference.

☐ My donation does not qualify for Gift Aid.

Please notify BRF if you want to cancel this Gift Aid declaration, change your name or home address, or no longer pay sufficient tax on your income and/or capital gains.

Please complete other side of form ➴

SHARING OUR VISION – MAKING A ONE-OFF GIFT

Please accept my gift of:

☐ £2 ☐ £5 ☐ £10 ☐ £20 Other £ _____

by (*delete as appropriate*):

☐ Cheque/Charity Voucher payable to 'BRF'

☐ MasterCard/Visa/Debit card/Charity card

Name on card

Card no. ☐☐☐☐ ☐☐☐☐ ☐☐☐☐ ☐☐☐☐

Expires end ☐M☐M ☐Y☐Y Security code* ☐☐☐

*Last 3 digits on the reverse of the card
ESSENTIAL IN ORDER TO PROCESS
YOUR PAYMENT

Signature   Date

☐ I would like to leave a gift to BRF in my will.
Please send me further information.

For help or advice regarding making a gift, please contact
our fundraising team +44 (0)1865 462305

Your privacy

We will use your personal data to process this transaction.
From time to time we may send you information about
the work of BRF that we think may be of interest to you.
Our privacy policy is available at **brf.org.uk/privacy**.
Please contact us if you wish to discuss your mailing
preferences.

Registered with

FUNDRAISING
REGULATOR

↰ Please complete other side of form

Please return this form to 'Freepost BRF'
No other address information or stamp is needed

The Bible Reading Fellowship is a Registered Charity (233280)

Overleaf… Reading *New Daylight* in a group | Author profile |
Recommended reading | Order and subscription forms

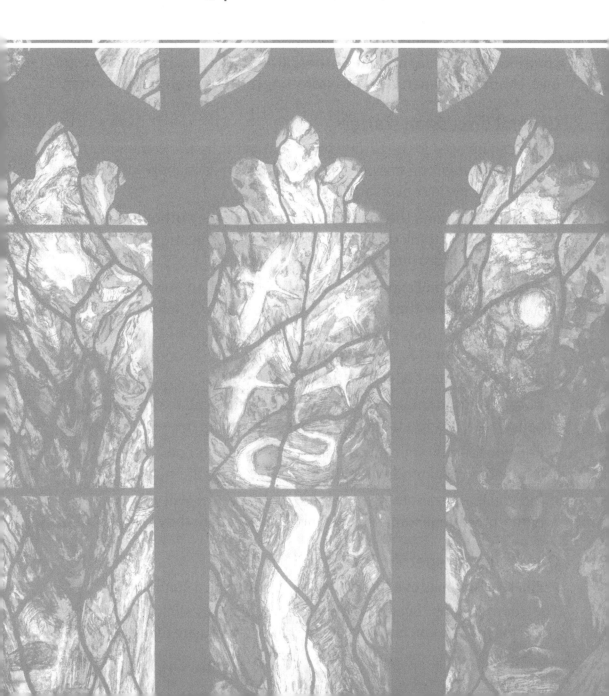

Reading *New Daylight* in a group

SALLY WELCH

I am aware that although some of you cherish the moments of quiet during the day which enable you to read and reflect on the passages we offer you in *New Daylight*, other readers prefer to study in small groups, to enable conversation and discussion and the sharing of insights. With this in mind, here are some ideas for discussion starters within a study group. Some of the questions are generic and can be applied to any set of contributions within this issue; others are specific to certain sets of readings. I hope they generate some interesting reflections and conversations!

General discussion starters

These can be used for any study series within this issue. Remember there are no right or wrong answers – these questions are simply to enable a group to engage in conversation.

- What do you think the main idea or theme of the author in this series? Do you think they succeeded in communicating this to you, or were you more interested in the side issues?

- Have you had any experience of the issues that are raised in the study? How have they affected your life?

- What evidence does the author use to support their ideas? Do they use personal observations and experience, facts, quotations from other authorities? Which appeals to you most?

- Does the author make a 'call to action'? Is that call realistic and achievable? Do you think their ideas will work in the secular world?

- Can you identify specific passages that struck you personally – as interesting, profound, difficult to understand or illuminating?

- Did you learn something new reading this series? Will you think differently about some things, and if so, what are they?

Questions for specific series

Psalm 43—56: songs of a threatened people (Veronica Zundel)

This set of psalms covers a wide range of emotions. Which one strikes a chord for you? Do you find it easier to pray when you are rejoicing or when you are anxious? For what or whom do you pray most often? Should you be changing this, and how might you do so?

Growing old (David Runcorn)

What has been your experience of ageing? What are the advantages and disadvantages, and does one outweigh the other?

David writes, 'My deepest struggle may not, after all, be with my sin and waywardness (though these are real). It may instead lie in accepting the extraordinary love with which God chooses to love me in all my dustiness and in trusting what he will yet reveal of who I truly am in his sight.' Is this your experience? How easy have you found this to do?

David explores the concept of 'Hello to here'. What do you think about this? How helpful might you find it?

Worship (a holy habit) (Paul Gravelle)

Paul writes that worship is a two-way communication. Has this been your experience? If not, what do you think has prevented this?

Reflect on the different styles of worship you have experienced over the years – how helpful have they been for you? Has the way you worship changed over time? Why do you think this is?

Paul tells us that when Jesus returns, 'it will be a worship occasion like none other'. What might it be like? Who would be involved? What would we all do?

1 and 2 Timothy (Jane Walters)

Give proper recognition to those widows who are really in need. But if a widow has children or grandchildren, these should learn first of all to put their religion into practice by caring for their own family and so repaying their parents and grandparents, for this is pleasing to God… Anyone who does not provide for their relatives, and especially for their own household, has denied the faith and is worse than an unbeliever.
1 TIMOTHY 5:3–4, 8 (NIV)

Mother Teresa is said to have told one man who asked her what he could do to help her cause: 'If you want to bring peace to the world, go home and love your family.' In what ways might you love your church family better?

Meet the author: Jane Walters

Jane, you include in your biography that you lead Christian creative writing retreats. What form do they take, and in what ways does a Christian writing retreat differ from a secular one?

We gather in a Christian hotel or conference centre for up to five days, enjoying improving our technique in morning sessions and experimenting in our own time during the afternoons. We spend the evenings sharing what we've written, ending the day with a short devotional time. Delegates range from complete beginners to published and award-winning authors of all genres. Age is no barrier. Our oldest has been 92! The Christian context includes praying together and sometimes using Bible stories as inspiration. Far more, though, is the premise that God has put a desire within us to write; and great freedom, joy and satisfaction can come when we do.

You have written a book about miscarriage. That must have been a very challenging task. How did you set about it?

Too Soon: A mother's journey through miscarriage (SPCK, 2018) came about through meeting a member of the **care.org** team at a Christian event. In many ways, it wasn't a difficult book to write. I knew the topic only too well from my own experience, and the difficulties I faced are common to most women in this situation. Since my aim was to offer comfort, help and hope, the greater challenge was to handle it all with sensitivity and empathy.

What advice would you give to anyone wanting to begin writing themselves?

People often tell me they'd like to write, and I always respond with the same advice. First, just start! Whether you pitch in at the beginning, middle or end of your story, get some words on the page. It can always be changed later. Second, join a writing group. Being with other writers has been the single biggest boost to my own writing.

Apart from writing, what gives you joy?

I teach music lessons at home and also perform on the saxophone. Additionally, I love making my own clothes, whether knitted or sewn. My favourite pastime is to cut up old garments and create new pieces unique to me. It saves the planet and my sanity!

Recommended reading

Environmental sustainability is a major issue for us all. In this extensively updated edition, Martin and Margot Hodson consider eight key environmental issues: biodiversity; climate change; water; population and consumption; energy; soil; food; and environment and development. Through ethical reflections, Bible studies on a different biblical doctrine for each chapter and eco-tips to enable a practical response, they outline the biblical basis for care of the environment and help the reader integrate environmental thinking and Christian faith.

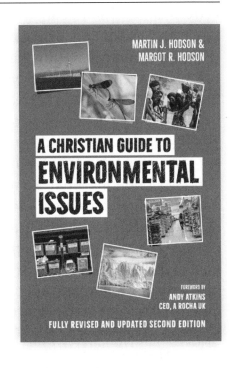

MARTIN J. HODSON & MARGOT R. HODSON

A CHRISTIAN GUIDE TO **ENVIRONMENTAL ISSUES**

FOREWORD BY ANDY ATKINS CEO, A ROCHA UK

FULLY REVISED AND UPDATED SECOND EDITION

The following is an edited extract taken from the final chapter of the book, entitled 'A covenant for hope'.

The People's Climate March 2014

On 20 and 21 September 2014 a coalition of organisations arranged climate change marches around the world just before world leaders were due to meet to discuss the issue at the United Nations. The New York meeting was itself a step along the way to the COP21 meeting in Paris in December 2015, at which a global agreement on cutting carbon emissions was due to be signed. Preparations were made for six months before the People's Climate March.

The biggest march was always going to be in New York itself (it was estimated at 310,000 people). In the week beforehand the then general secretary of the UN, Ban Ki-moon, announced that he would be on the New York march, and he was joined by Christiana Figueres, executive secretary of the UN Framework Convention on Climate Change (UNFCCC), Al Gore, former vice-president of the USA, and the actor Leonardo DiCaprio.

In London, The Climate Coalition organised the biggest (approximately 40,000 people) of several marches in the UK, and those present included the actress Emma Thompson, the singer Peter Gabriel and Richard Chartres, the bishop of London, who gave a powerful speech at the rally.

In September 2014 we were on our sabbatical trip in the Sierra Nevada, Spain. We decided to make every effort to go on a march. We checked on the web, expecting that the nearest march would involve a bus journey into Granada, but we had a surprise when we discovered a march in Portugos, a village just a short walk down the road from Pitres where we were staying. We rather expected that the numbers would be small, and set off on the Sunday wondering what we would find. When we got to Portugos it was not easy to find the march, and we did quite a lot of marching just to do so! But eventually we found a brave group of environmentalists bearing two posters saying 'Si el clima es muy fragil tambien tu $' ('If the climate is very fragile, so are your dollars'). There were 13 of us and four dogs, so not quite on the scale of New York or London. We took photos of our march outside the town hall and then went to a bar afterwards for a drink and a chat.

There were thought to be 600,000 people on the marches worldwide, but did they have any impact? We are not sure, but they are a sign of hope. Two days later at the Climate Summit in New York, US President Barack Obama at least acknowledged the marches: 'So the climate is changing faster than our efforts to address it. The alarm bells keep ringing. Our citizens keep marching. We cannot pretend we do not hear them.'

Climate strikes

Obama was right and the citizens have kept marching. But it was probably not the ones he expected.

I (Martin) use Twitter quite a lot. For me it is not something I play with but a useful research tool. If you follow the right people and organisations it is possible to find out a lot of useful information, sometimes a long way ahead of the crowd. Back in autumn 2018, I spotted something unusual. A young Swedish girl called Greta Thunberg seemed to be gathering quite a following with her weekly strikes, 'Friday for the future'.

Greta started her strikes outside the Swedish parliament building on 20 August 2018. They soon grew to an international youth movement. I first saw a small strike of school children in Oxford in January 2019, and throughout that year there was a phenomenal growth in the movement. Greta became a celebrity and was invited to speak all over the world. She took two daring trans-Atlantic trips on yachts from Europe to the United States and back. Throughout 2019 and early 2020 there was a huge amount of activity. Greta's speeches were turned into a book. In January 2019, at the World Economic Forum in Davos, she ended her speech with:

Adults keep saying, 'We owe it to young people to give them hope.' But I don't want your hope. I don't want you to be hopeful. I want you to panic. I want you to feel the fear I feel every day, and then I want you to act. I want you to act as you would in a crisis. I want you to act as if our house is on fire. Because it is.

We know what Greta means, and we desperately want people to take action; there is a false hope that leads to complacency. But there is a place for real hope, not thrust on to young people, but to keep each of us going in what can be very disheartening times. And there is a place for Christian hope. In this final chapter we will look at some projects that inspire hope, and at what the Bible has to say about hope.

To order a copy of this book, please use the order form on page 151 or visit **brfonline.org.uk***.*

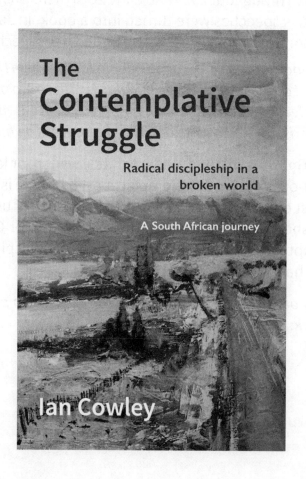

The Contemplative Struggle

Radical discipleship in a broken world

A South African journey

Ian Cowley

In *The Contemplative Struggle*, Ian Cowley sets the central themes of John's gospel alongside each other – abiding in Christ, conflict, light and darkness, obedience, loving one another – and explores how these can be reconciled in daily life. Drawing on his experience of living in his native South Africa during the apartheid era and challenging understandings of contemplative spirituality as essentially inward discipline, he highlights the urgent need for Christians to be active in transforming a suffering world.

The Contemplative Struggle
Radical discipleship in a broken world
Ian Cowley
978 0 085746 982 3 £8.99
brfonline.org.uk

To order

Online: **brfonline.org.uk**
Telephone: +44 (0)1865 319700
Mon–Fri 9.30–17.00

Delivery times within the UK are normally 15 working days. Prices are correct at the time of going to press but may change without prior notice.

Title	Price	Qty	Total
A Christian Guide to Environmental Issues (second edition)	£9.99		
The Contemplative Struggle	£8.99		

POSTAGE AND PACKING CHARGES			
Order value	UK	Europe	Rest of world
Under £7.00	£2.00	Available on request	Available on request
£7.00–£29.99	£3.00		
£30.00 and over	FREE		

Total value of books	
Postage and packing	
Donation*	
Total for this order	

* Please complete and return the Gift Aid declaration on page 141.

Please complete in BLOCK CAPITALS

Title _____ First name/initials _____ Surname _____

Address _____

_____ Postcode _____

Acc. No. _____ Telephone _____

Email _____

Method of payment

❏ Cheque (made payable to BRF) ❏ MasterCard / Visa

Card no. ▢▢▢▢ ▢▢▢▢ ▢▢▢▢ ▢▢▢▢

Expires end ▢M▢M ▢Y▢Y Security code* ▢▢▢ Last 3 digits on the reverse of the card

Signature* _____ Date _____/_____/_____

*ESSENTIAL IN ORDER TO PROCESS YOUR ORDER

Please return this form to:
BRF, 15 The Chambers, Vineyard, Abingdon OX14 3FE | **enquiries@brf.org.uk**
To read our terms and find out about cancelling your order, please visit **brfonline.org.uk/terms**.

The Bible Reading Fellowship (BRF) is a Registered Charity (233280)

BRF needs you!

If you're one of our many thousands of regular *New Daylight* readers, you will know all about the benefits and blessings of regular Bible reading and the value of daily notes to guide, inform and inspire you.

Here are some recent comments from *New Daylight* readers:

> *'Thank you for all the many inspiring writings that help so much when things are tough.'*

> *'Just right for me – I learned a lot!'*

> *'We looked forward to each day's message as we pondered each passage and comment.'*

If you have similarly positive things to say about *New Daylight*, would you be willing to share your experience with others? Could you ask for a brief slot during church notices or write a short piece for your church magazine or website? Do you belong to groups, formal or informal, where you could share your experience of using Bible reading notes and encourage others to try them?

It doesn't need to be complicated or nerve-wracking; just answering these three questions in what you say or write will get your message across:

- How do Bible reading notes help you grow in your faith?
- Where, when and how do you use them?
- What would you say to people who don't already use them?

We can supply further information if you need it and would love to hear about it if you do give a talk or write an article.

For more information:

- Email **enquiries@brf.org.uk**
- Telephone BRF on +44 (0)1865 319700 Mon–Fri 9.30–17.00
- Write to us at BRF, 15 The Chambers, Vineyard, Abingdon OX14 3FE

Enabling all ages to grow in faith

At BRF, we long for people of all ages to grow in faith and understanding of the Bible. That's what all our work as a charity is about.

- Our **Living Faith** range of resources helps Christians go deeper in their understanding of scripture, in prayer and in their walk with God. Our conferences and events bring people together to share this journey, while our Holy Habits resources help whole congregations grow together as disciples of Jesus, living out and sharing their faith.

- We also want to make it easier for local churches to engage effectively in ministry and mission – by helping them bring new families into a growing relationship with God through **Messy Church** or by supporting churches as they nurture the spiritual life of older people through **Anna Chaplaincy**.

- Our **Parenting for Faith** team coaches parents and others to raise God-connected children and teens, and enables churches to fully support them.

Do you share our vision?

Though a significant proportion of BRF's funding is generated through our charitable activities, we are dependent on the generous support of individuals, churches and charitable trusts.

If you share our vision, would you help us to enable even more people of all ages to grow in faith? Your prayers and financial support are vital for the work that we do. You could:

- Support BRF's ministry with a regular donation;
- Support us with a one-off gift;
- Consider leaving a gift to BRF in your will (see page 154);
- Encourage your church to support BRF as part of your church's giving to home mission – perhaps focusing on a specific ministry or programme;
- Most important of all, support BRF with your prayers.

Donate at **brf.org.uk/donate** or use the form on pages 141–42.

God at work in the ordinary every day, from one generation to the next...

Hear, O Israel: The Lord our God, the Lord is one... These commandments that I give you today are to be on your hearts. Impress them on your children. Talk about them when you sit at home and when you walk along the road, when you lie down and when you get up.

DEUTERONOMY 6:4–7 (NIV, abridged)

Two things strike me here. First, there is the plurality to the commands given. It is not 'Hear, O parents' or 'Hear, O children's workers' but 'Hear, O Israel'. Today, parents are primarily responsible for raising their children in the faith, but the whole community has a part to play. The children of the church are 'our' children.

Second, there is a beauty to *how* we are to impress God's commands on the next generation. We are to talk when at home, when away, when we get up and when we lie down. Our task, whether or not we have our own children, is to live out our faith and let 'our' children see in our daily lives.

parenting for faith®

Through Parenting for Faith, BRF works to resource and empower parents, carers, and churches in raising children in the faith. We strive to support as many as we can and give what we offer freely.

This is only possible because of generous donations from donors, churches, charitable trusts, and gifts in wills.

We would love your support. You can find out more about Parenting for Faith at **brf.org.uk/parentingforfaith**. If you can support this ministry financially, please consider whether you could give a regular gift. You can find out how to give regularly via **brf.org.uk/friends** or get in touch with us on **01235 462305** or via **giving@brf.org.uk**.

Your prayers, as ever, are hugely appreciated.

> Pray. Give. Get involved.
> **brf.org.uk**

NEW DAYLIGHT SUBSCRIPTION RATES

Please note our new subscription rates, current until 30 April 2022:

Individual subscriptions
covering 3 issues for under 5 copies, payable in advance
(including postage & packing):

	UK	Europe	Rest of world
New Daylight	£18.00	£25.95	£29.85
New Daylight 3-year subscription (9 issues) (not available for Deluxe)	£52.65	N/A	N/A
New Daylight Deluxe per set of 3 issues p.a.	£22.35	£32.55	£38.55

Group subscriptions
covering 3 issues for 5 copies or more, sent to one UK address (post free):

New Daylight	£14.25 per set of 3 issues p.a.
New Daylight Deluxe	£17.85 per set of 3 issues p.a.

Please note that the annual billing period for group subscriptions runs from 1 May to 30 April.

Overseas group subscription rates
Available on request. Please email **enquiries@brf.org.uk**.

Copies may also be obtained from Christian bookshops:

New Daylight	£4.75 per copy
New Daylight Deluxe	£5.95 per copy

All our Bible reading notes can be ordered online by visiting
brfonline.org.uk/subscriptions

New Daylight
New Daylight is also available as an app for
Android, iPhone and iPad
brfonline.org.uk/apps

NEW DAYLIGHT INDIVIDUAL SUBSCRIPTION FORM

All our Bible reading notes can be ordered online by visiting
brfonline.org.uk/subscriptions

☐ I would like to take out a subscription:

Title _____ First name/initials _____ Surname _____

Address _____

_____ Postcode _____

Telephone _____ Email _____

Please send *New Daylight* beginning with the September 2021 / January 2022 / May 2022 issue (*delete as appropriate*):

(*please tick box*)	UK	Europe	Rest of world
New Daylight 1-year subscription	☐ £18.00	☐ £25.95	☐ £29.85
New Daylight 3-year subscription	☐ £52.65	N/A	N/A
New Daylight Deluxe	☐ £22.35	☐ £32.55	☐ £38.55

Optional donation to support the work of BRF £ _____

Total enclosed £ _____ (cheques should be made payable to 'BRF')

Please complete and return the Gift Aid declaration on page 141 to make your donation even more valuable to us.

Please charge my MasterCard / Visa ☐ Debit card ☐ with £ _____

Card no. ☐☐☐☐ ☐☐☐☐ ☐☐☐☐ ☐☐☐☐

Expires end ☐M ☐M ☐Y ☐Y Security code* ☐☐☐ Last 3 digits on the reverse of the card

Signature* _____ Date _____ /_____ /_____

*ESSENTIAL IN ORDER TO PROCESS YOUR PAYMENT

To set up a Direct Debit, please also complete the Direct Debit instruction on page 159 and return it to BRF with this form.

Please return this form with the appropriate payment to:
BRF, 15 The Chambers, Vineyard, Abingdon OX14 3FE

To read our terms and find out about cancelling your order, please visit **brfonline.org.uk/terms**.

The Bible Reading Fellowship is a Registered Charity (233280)

ND0221

NEW DAYLIGHT GIFT SUBSCRIPTION FORM

☐ I would like to give a gift subscription (please provide both names and addresses):

Title _____ First name/initials _____ Surname _____

Address _____

_____ Postcode _____

Telephone _____ Email _____

Gift subscription name _____

Gift subscription address _____

_____ Postcode _____

Gift message (20 words max. or include your own gift card):

_____

_____

Please send *New Daylight* beginning with the September 2021 / January 2022 / May 2022 issue (*delete as appropriate*):

(*please tick box*)	UK	Europe	Rest of world
New Daylight 1-year subscription	☐ £18.00	☐ £25.95	☐ £29.85
New Daylight 3-year subscription	☐ £52.65	N/A	N/A
New Daylight Deluxe	☐ £22.35	☐ £32.55	☐ £38.55

Optional donation to support the work of BRF £ _____

Total enclosed £ _____ (cheques should be made payable to 'BRF')

Please complete and return the Gift Aid declaration on page 141 to make your donation even more valuable to us.

Please charge my MasterCard / Visa ☐ Debit card ☐ with £ _____

Card no. ☐☐☐☐ ☐☐☐☐ ☐☐☐☐ ☐☐☐☐

Expires end ☐☐ ☐☐   Security code* ☐☐☐   Last 3 digits on the reverse of the card

Signature* _____ Date _____/_____/_____

*ESSENTIAL IN ORDER TO PROCESS YOUR PAYMENT

To set up a Direct Debit, please also complete the Direct Debit instruction on page 159 and return it to BRF with this form.

Please return this form with the appropriate payment to:
BRF, 15 The Chambers, Vineyard, Abingdon OX14 3FE

To read our terms and find out about cancelling your order, please visit **brfonline.org.uk/terms**.

The Bible Reading Fellowship is a Registered Charity (233280)

You can pay for your annual subscription to our Bible reading notes using Direct Debit. You need only give your bank details once, and the payment is made automatically every year until you cancel it. If you would like to pay by Direct Debit, please use the form opposite, entering your BRF account number under 'Reference number'.

You are fully covered by the Direct Debit Guarantee:

The Direct Debit Guarantee

- This Guarantee is offered by all banks and building societies that accept instructions to pay Direct Debits.

- If there are any changes to the amount, date or frequency of your Direct Debit, The Bible Reading Fellowship will notify you 10 working days in advance of your account being debited or as otherwise agreed. If you request The Bible Reading Fellowship to collect a payment, confirmation of the amount and date will be given to you at the time of the request.

- If an error is made in the payment of your Direct Debit, by The Bible Reading Fellowship or your bank or building society, you are entitled to a full and immediate refund of the amount paid from your bank or building society.

- If you receive a refund you are not entitled to, you must pay it back when The Bible Reading Fellowship asks you to.

- You can cancel a Direct Debit at any time by simply contacting your bank or building society. Written confirmation may be required. Please also notify us.

The Bible Reading Fellowship

Instruction to your bank or building society to pay by Direct Debit

Please fill in the whole form using a ballpoint pen and return it to:
BRF, 15 The Chambers, Vineyard, Abingdon OX14 3FE

Service User Number: | 5 | 5 | 8 | 2 | 2 | 9 |

Name and full postal address of your bank or building society

To: The Manager	Bank/Building Society
Address	
	Postcode

Name(s) of account holder(s)

Branch sort code

| | | - | | | - | | |

Bank/Building Society account number

| | | | | | | | |

Reference number

| | | | | | | |

Instruction to your Bank/Building Society

Please pay The Bible Reading Fellowship Direct Debits from the account detailed in this instruction, subject to the safeguards assured by the Direct Debit Guarantee. I understand that this instruction may remain with The Bible Reading Fellowship and, if so, details will be passed electronically to my bank/building society.

Signature(s)

Banks and Building Societies may not accept Direct Debit instructions for some types of account.

ND0221

Enabling all ages to grow in faith

Anna Chaplaincy

Living Faith

Messy Church

Parenting for Faith

The Bible Reading Fellowship (BRF) is a Christian charity that resources individuals and churches. Our vision is to enable people of all ages to grow in faith and understanding of the Bible and to see more people equipped to exercise their gifts in leadership and ministry.

To find out more about our ministries, visit

brf.org.uk